TRANSCENDING IMAGES

Art, Poetry

Transcending Images
(Art, Poetry)

Izya Shlosberg, Boris Kokotov

Book design by Izya Shlosberg

Cover design by Izya Shlosberg

Poetry Editor: Kendra Kopelke

How it has happened…

In May 2009, my old friend, renowned artist and writer Izya Shlosberg, called to tell me he was putting together a catalogue of his most recent work.

"Would you be interested in writing something for it?" he asked.

"Something like what? an endorsement? "

"Some poetry maybe…" Izya replied, and the same night emailed me the link to his paintings on www.artfact.net.

I looked through digitized images of these highly symbolic, playful, instantly recognizable works. Most of them I had already seen in his studio or in art galleries in Baltimore, Washington, D.C., and New York. As one critic put it, "Their complexity defies formulaic understanding..." and I might add that their evasive meaning resists any attempt to be captured by trivial descriptions or simplistic interpretations. It was clear to me that in order to become a legitimate companion to the art an accompanying text should convey my own ideas and be executed in my own style and technique.

Two months later, twenty six (I had to stop somewhere and decided that the "from A to Z" template was an excellent excuse) rather laconic verses have been written.

Interacting with the paintings' vast reservoir of notions and concepts was very exciting to me. What value the poems add to the paintings is up to public to decide. I would only state that to "transcend the images" isn't an easy task – but it is rewarding.

Boris Kokotov

July 2009

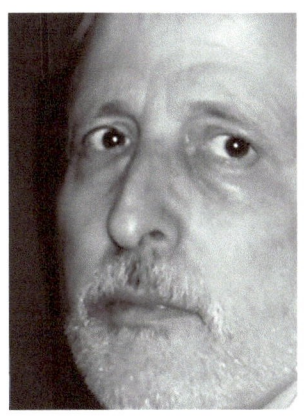

IZYA SHLOSBERG was born in the small town of Pinsk, Belarus, in 1950. He began painting at an early age, had his first art exhibition at age 13, and graduated from Moscow Art University in 1981. His paintings have been exhibited in Belarus, Russia, Ukraine, Hungary, Germany, Poland, Spain, Israel, and the United States. He is the well-known, prolific artist, having created over 500 works in the last decade, many of which are in museums, galleries and private collections. He moved to the United States in 1994 and currently lives in Baltimore, Maryland.

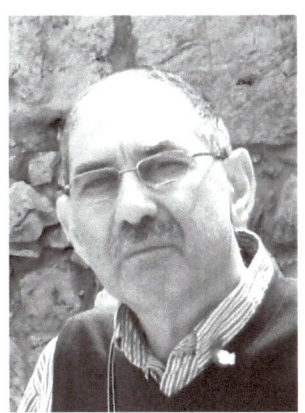

BORIS KOKOTOV, born in Moscow in 1946, is a poet, translator, and critic. His first collection of poetry, Prints, appeared in 1971. His poems have appeared in journals in the United States, Germany, Israel, and Russia. He is the author of five more collections of Russian poetry, The Night Bird, (1985) End of Quotation (1996), Material Evidence (1998), Shooting at a Moving Target (2000), and Air Traps (2006). He has translated several 19th and 20th century German poets into Russian and is the editor of a translation of R.M. Rilke's Sonnets to Orpheus (Moscow, 2008). Boris Kokotov is on the editorial board of the Russian/English annual literature journal Gostinnaya. He moved from Moscow to the United States in 1991. This is his first publication in English.

TRANSCENDING IMAGES

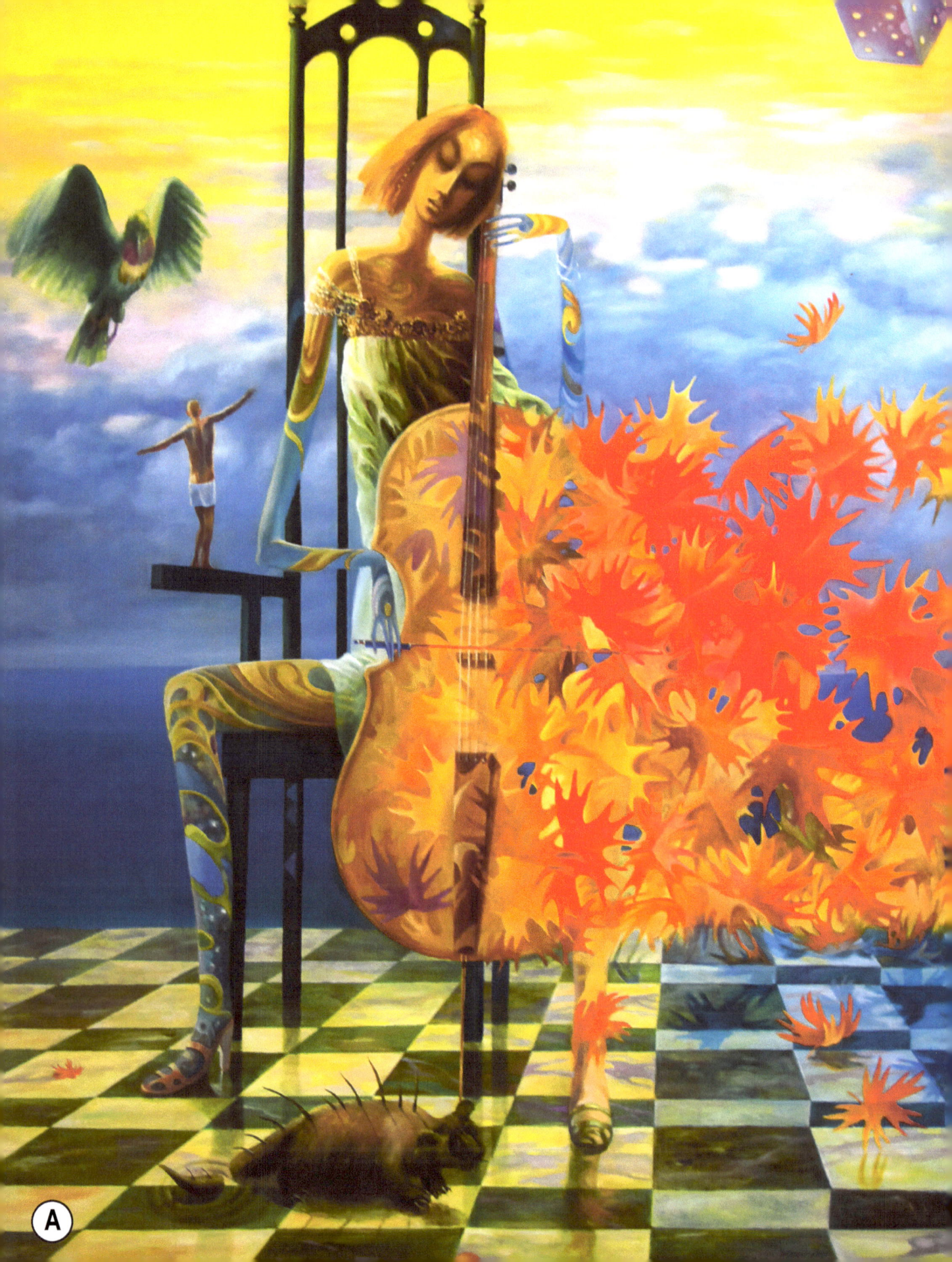

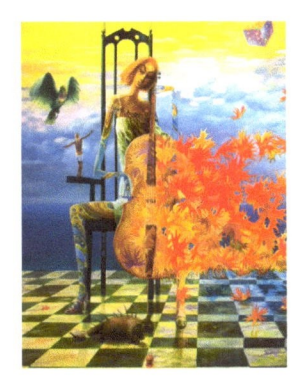

here is the dilemma:
to make a decision
or throw the dice.

wait a minute… – the bird sings.
what's the difference? – the cat murmurs.
it doesn't matter – the leaves whisper.

perhaps
playing the cello
is an option as well.

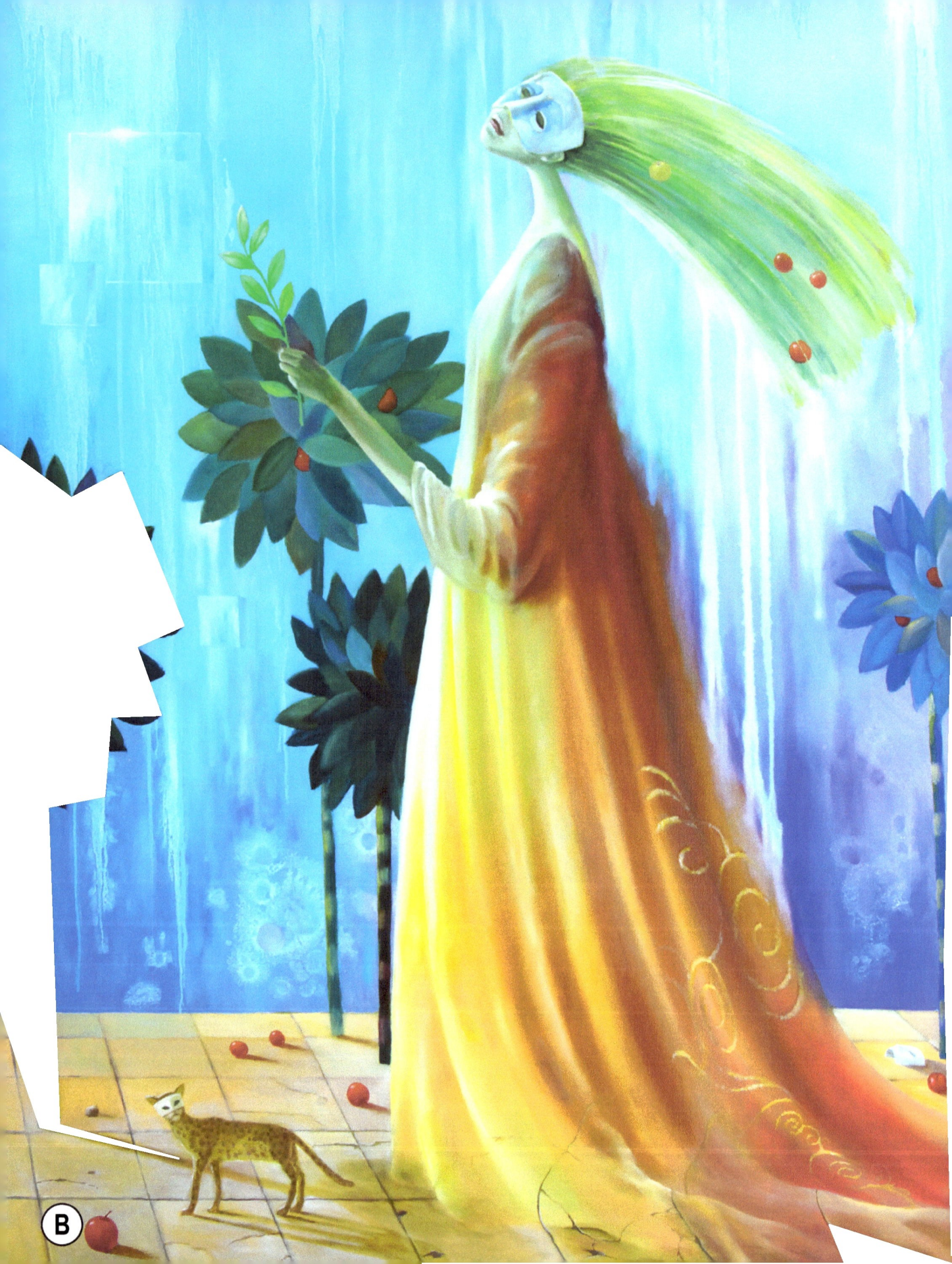

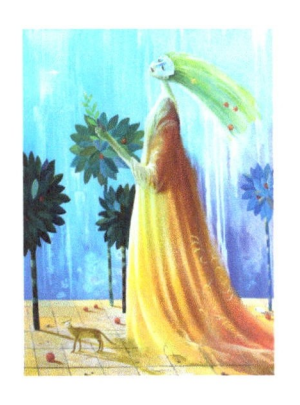

too many lives, you know,
too many castles
made of sad music.

do not trust a sailor though:
he has no regrets,
he knows nothing about reflection.

he is not your hero.

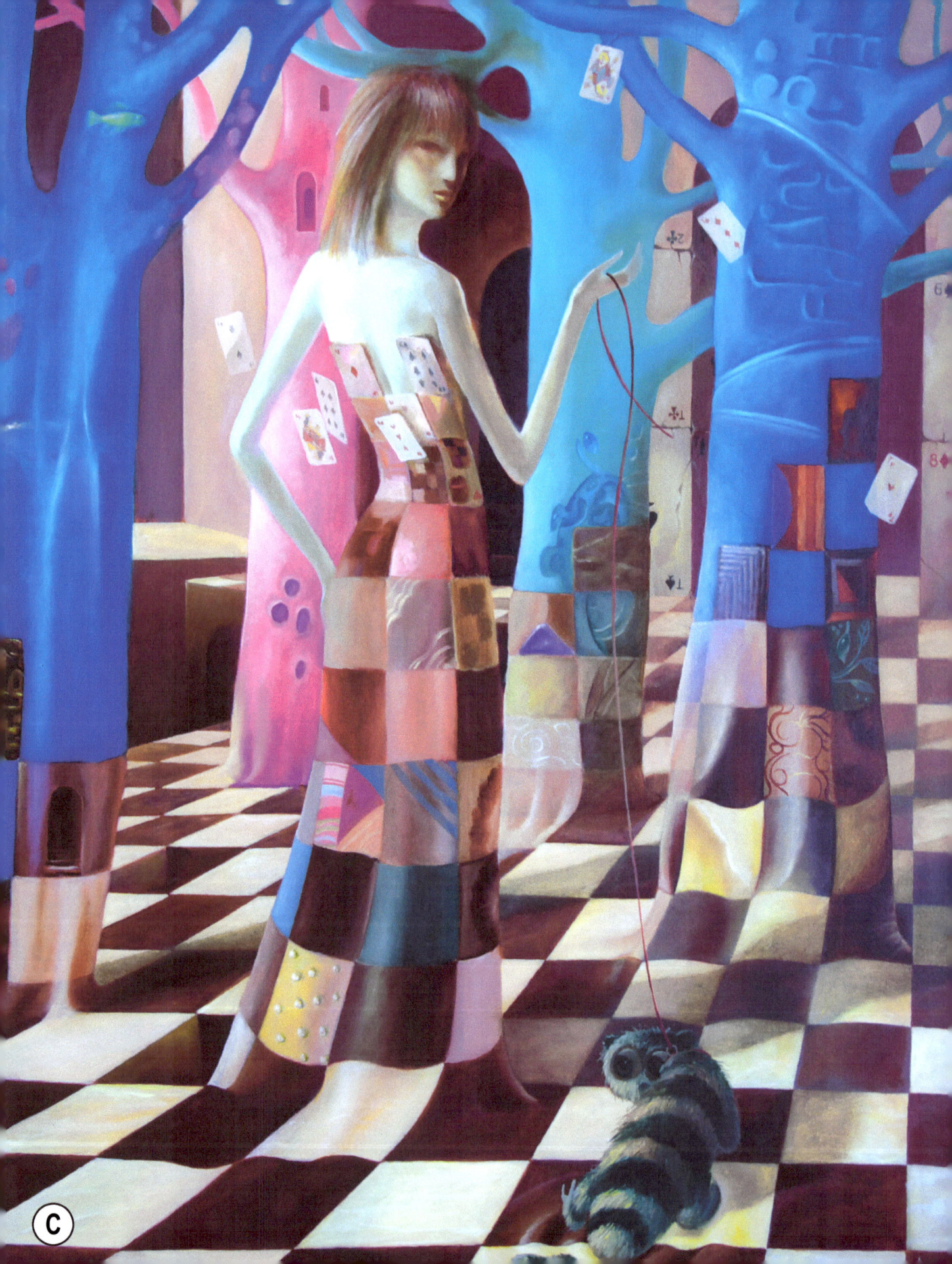

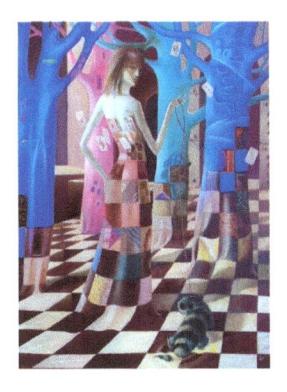

always concentrate
on what you are doing,

but when you walk your dog
be aware of what the dog is doing.

otherwise the neighbors,
those creatures of discontent,
might become offended.

(unless offending them
is your hidden agenda)

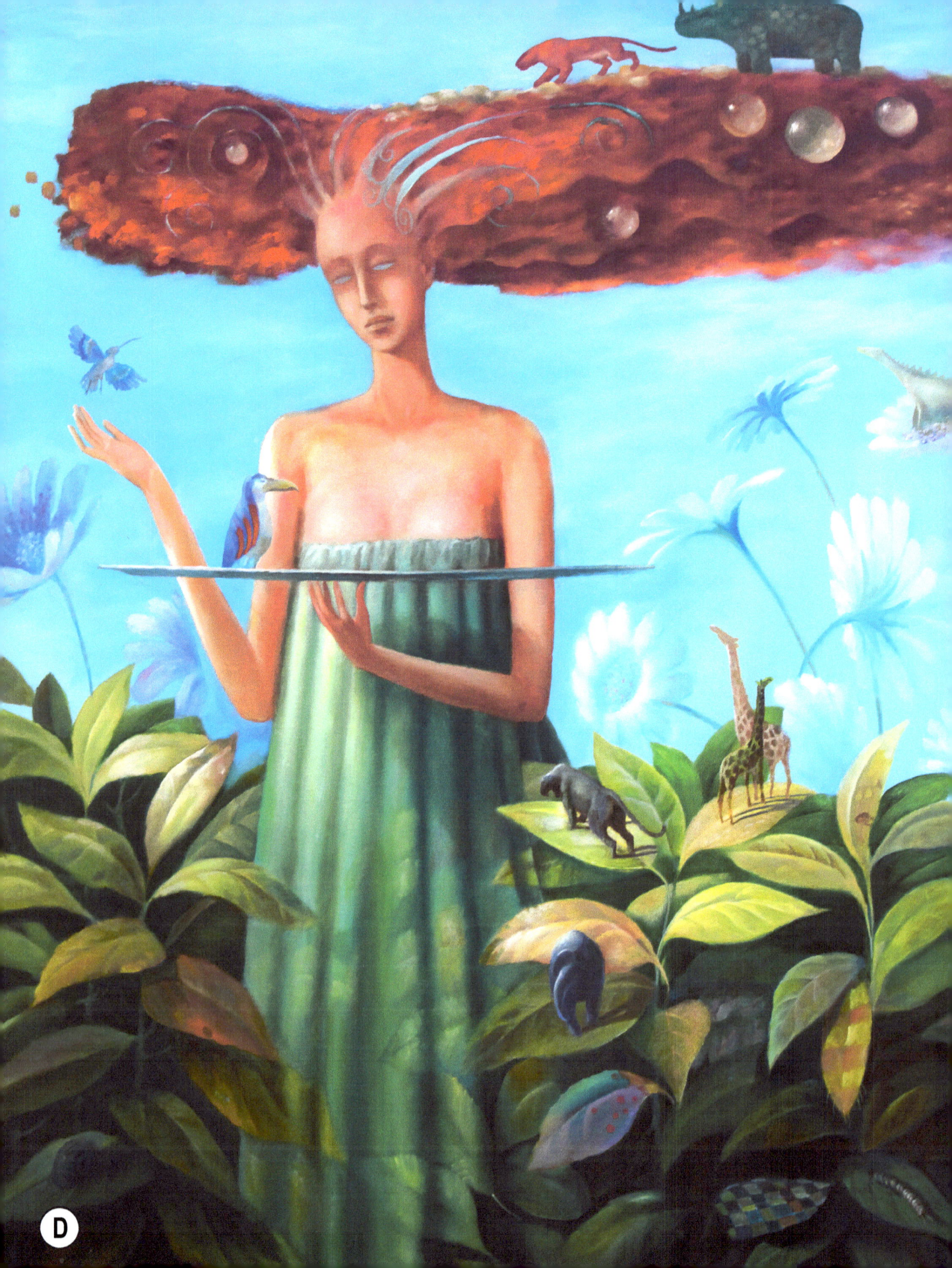

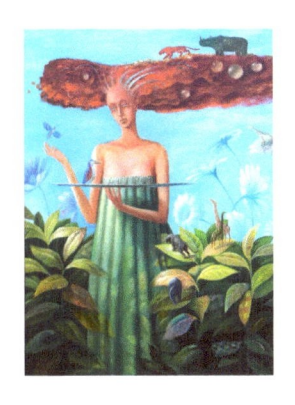

a few facts about birds –
descendants of dinosaurs:

they fly
they sing
they crap

right on the hood
of my shiny new car –
a descendant of the primordial wheel.

now, I've got reservations
about the course of evolution…

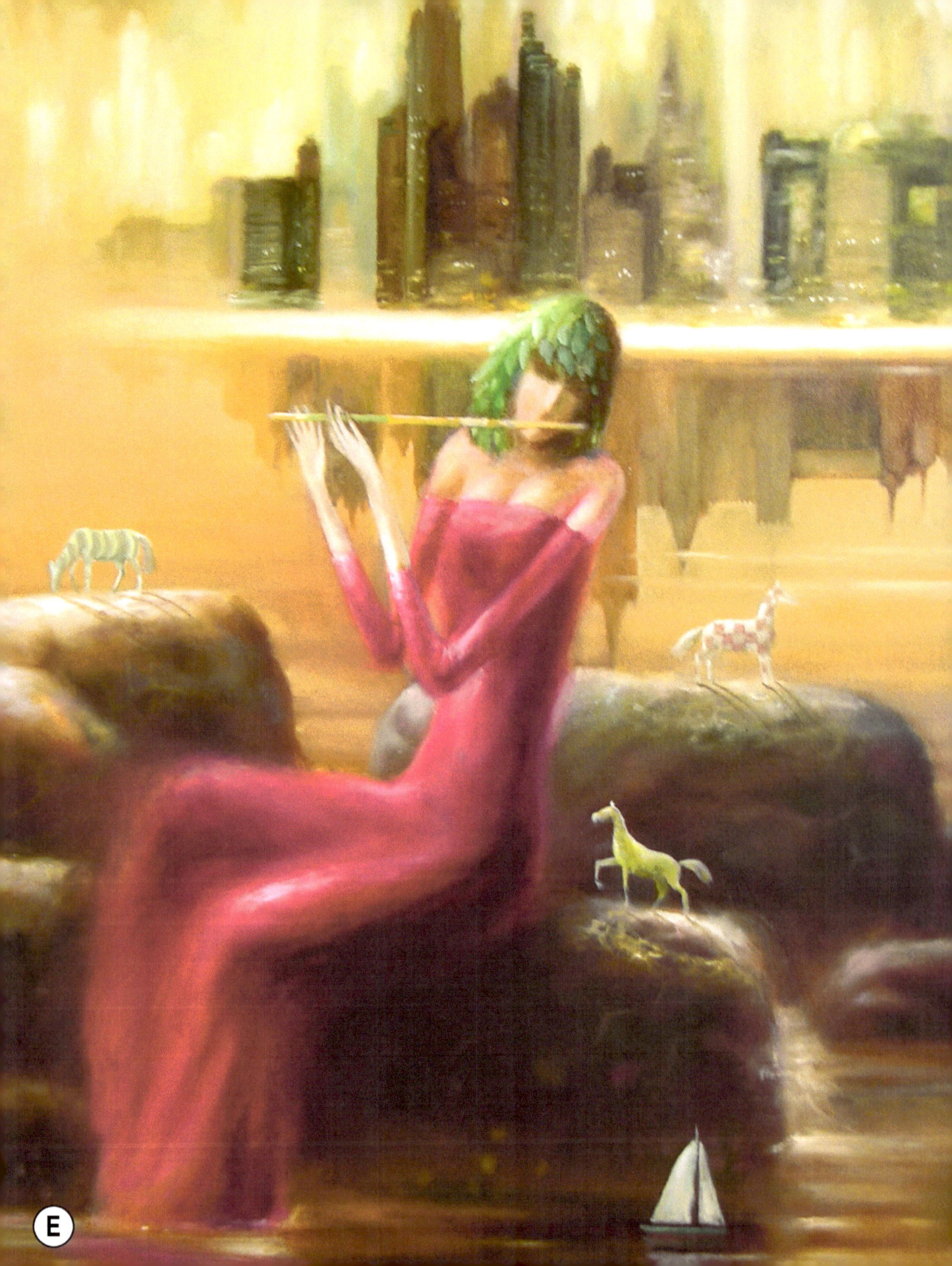

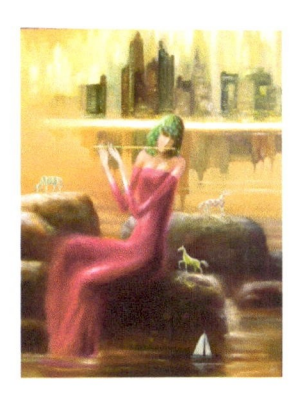

the flute was invented
long before
people were invented.

nothing magical about the flute –
a flimsy tube to tune
the planets' orbits.

nothing mysterious about people –
a clumsy tool to wreck the order
devised by the flute.

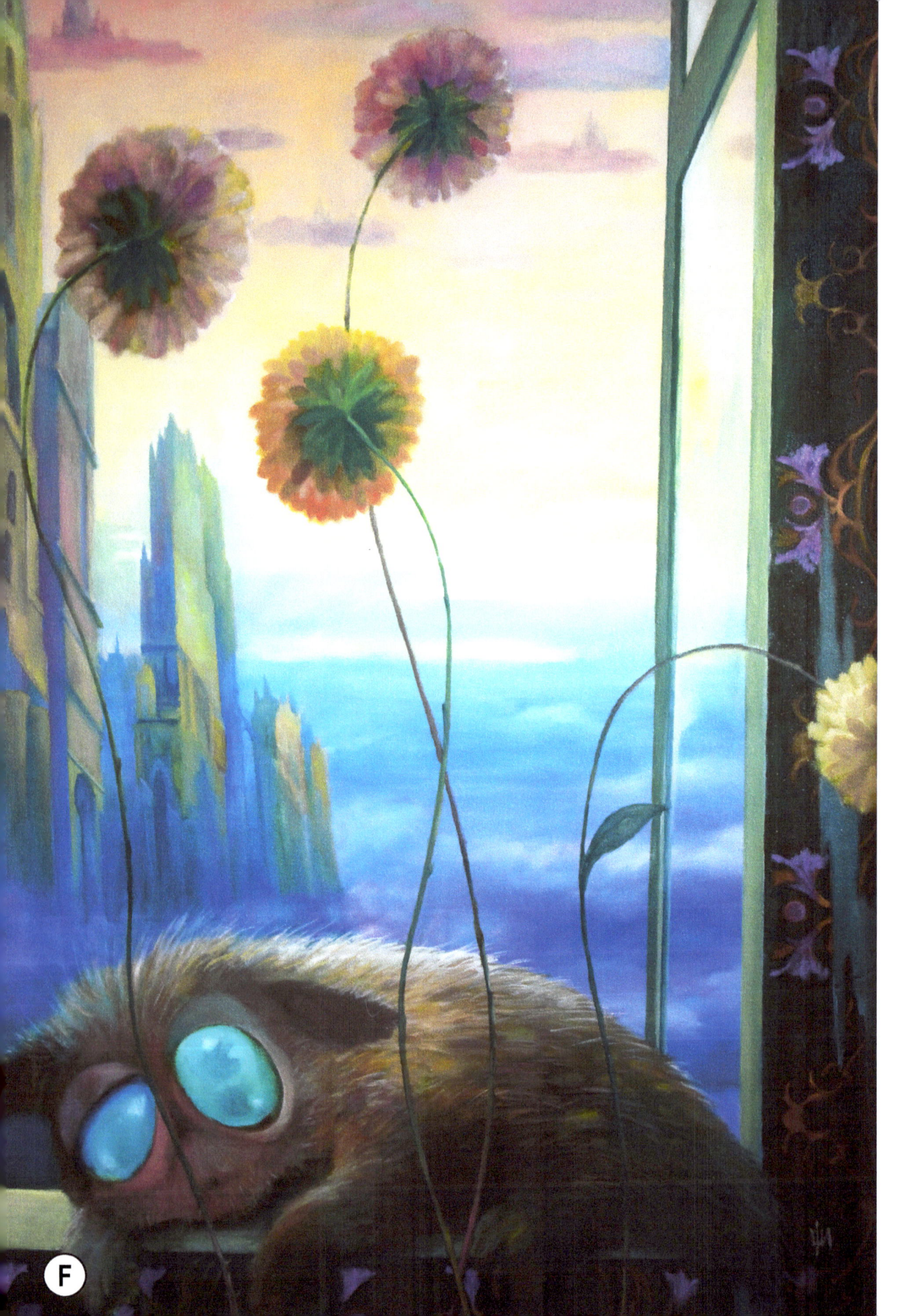

F

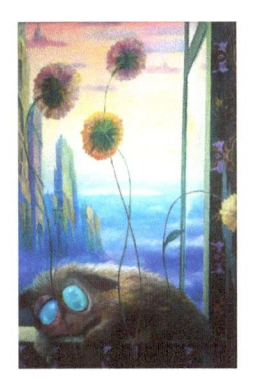

no comments on a deity
crossing the sky
in a magnificent chariot…

think about a sunflower
following a distant star
on its own schedule

as a curious observer,
a witness –
not a welfare recipient.

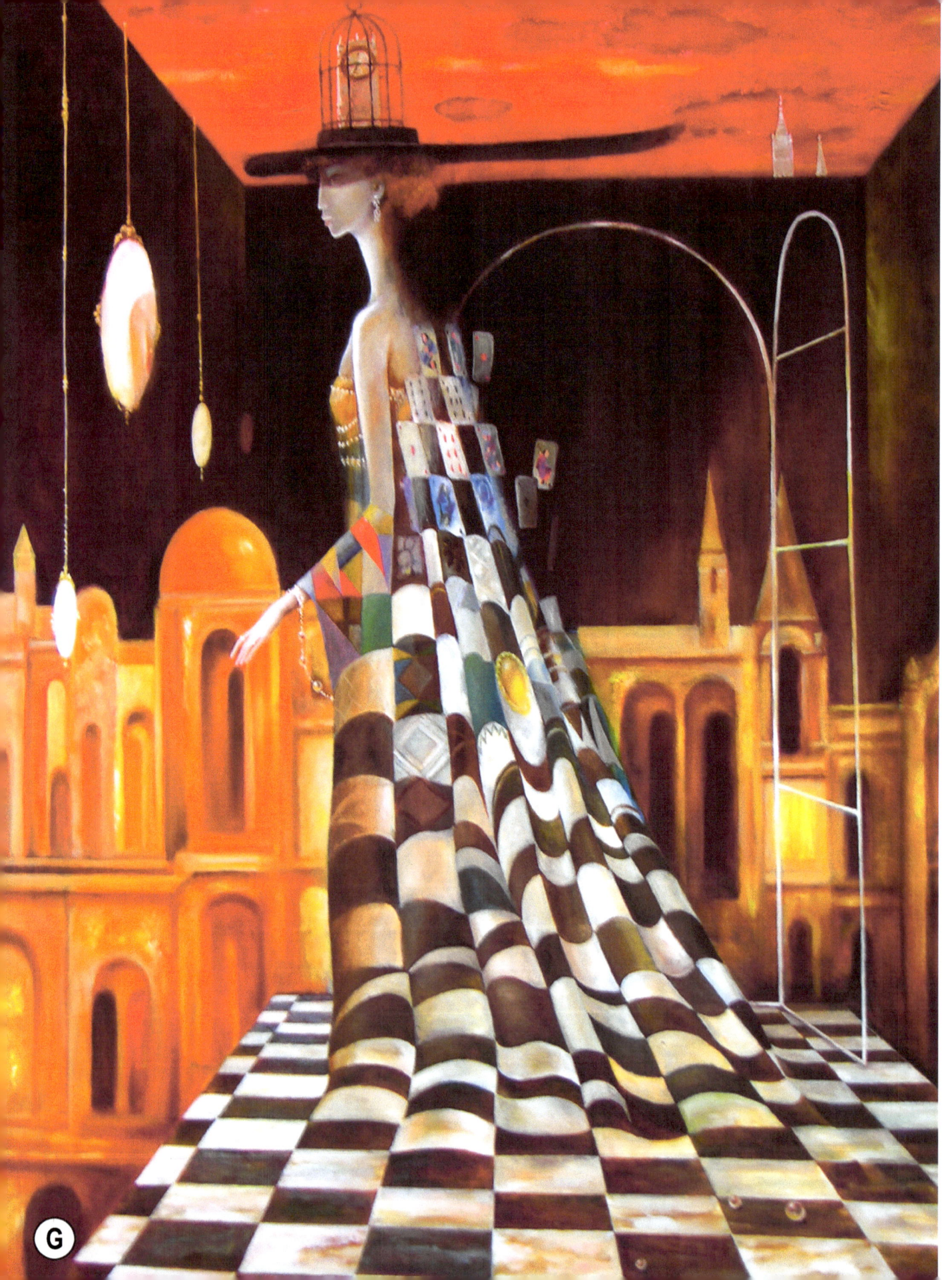

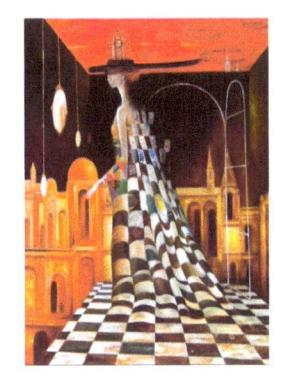

there are castles
that can not be entered
despite of our efforts.

silently transcending time
they induce us
to shift attention

and get lost
in our own
distortion of reality.

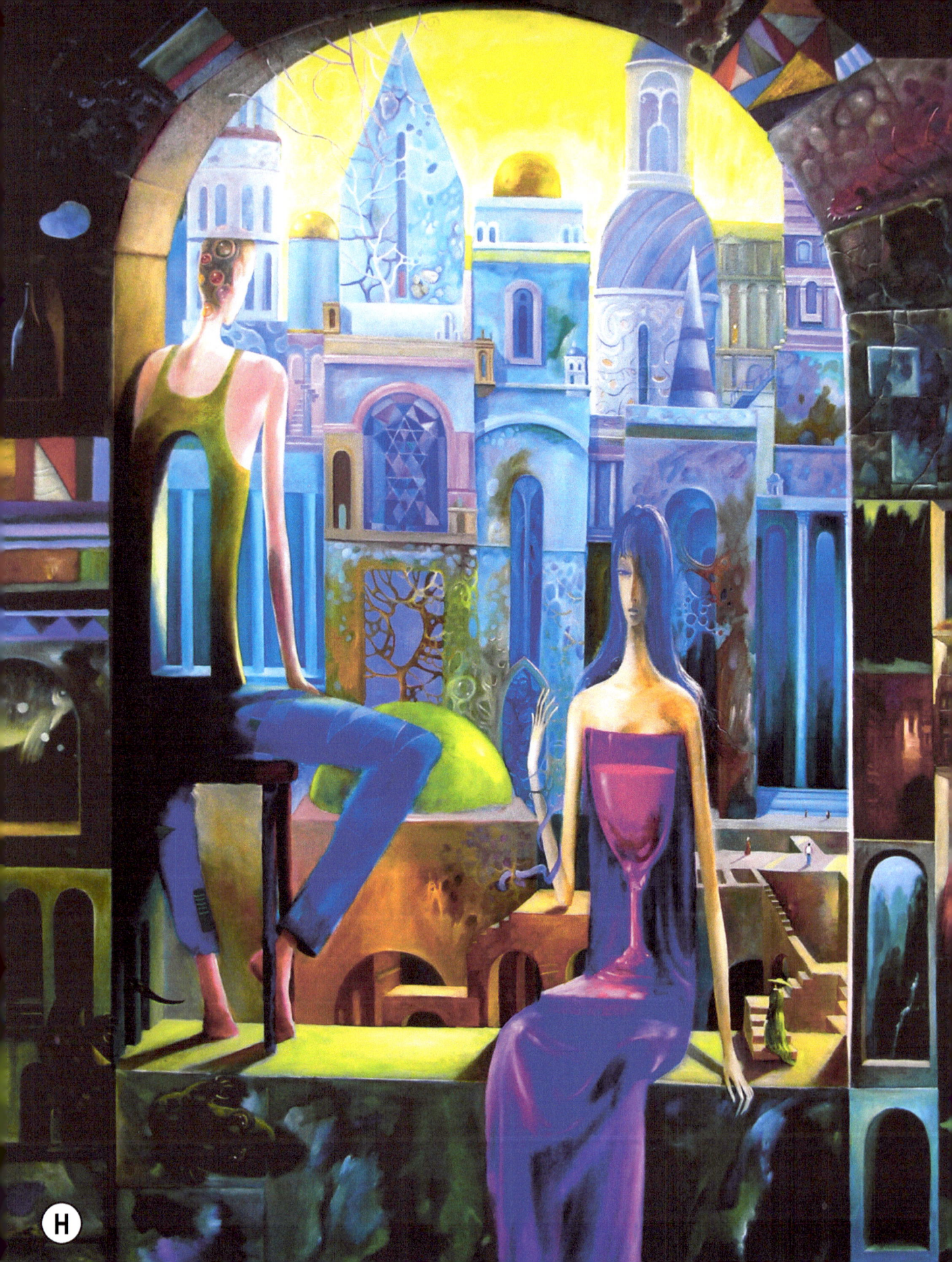

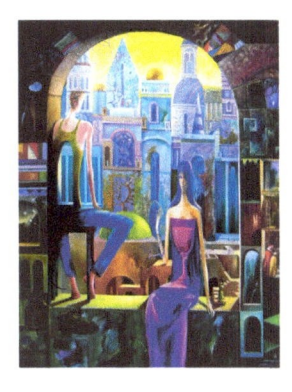

it does not matter
who came first
to build the tower.

destruction dwells
deep inside the builder.

we knew that
even before he vanished.

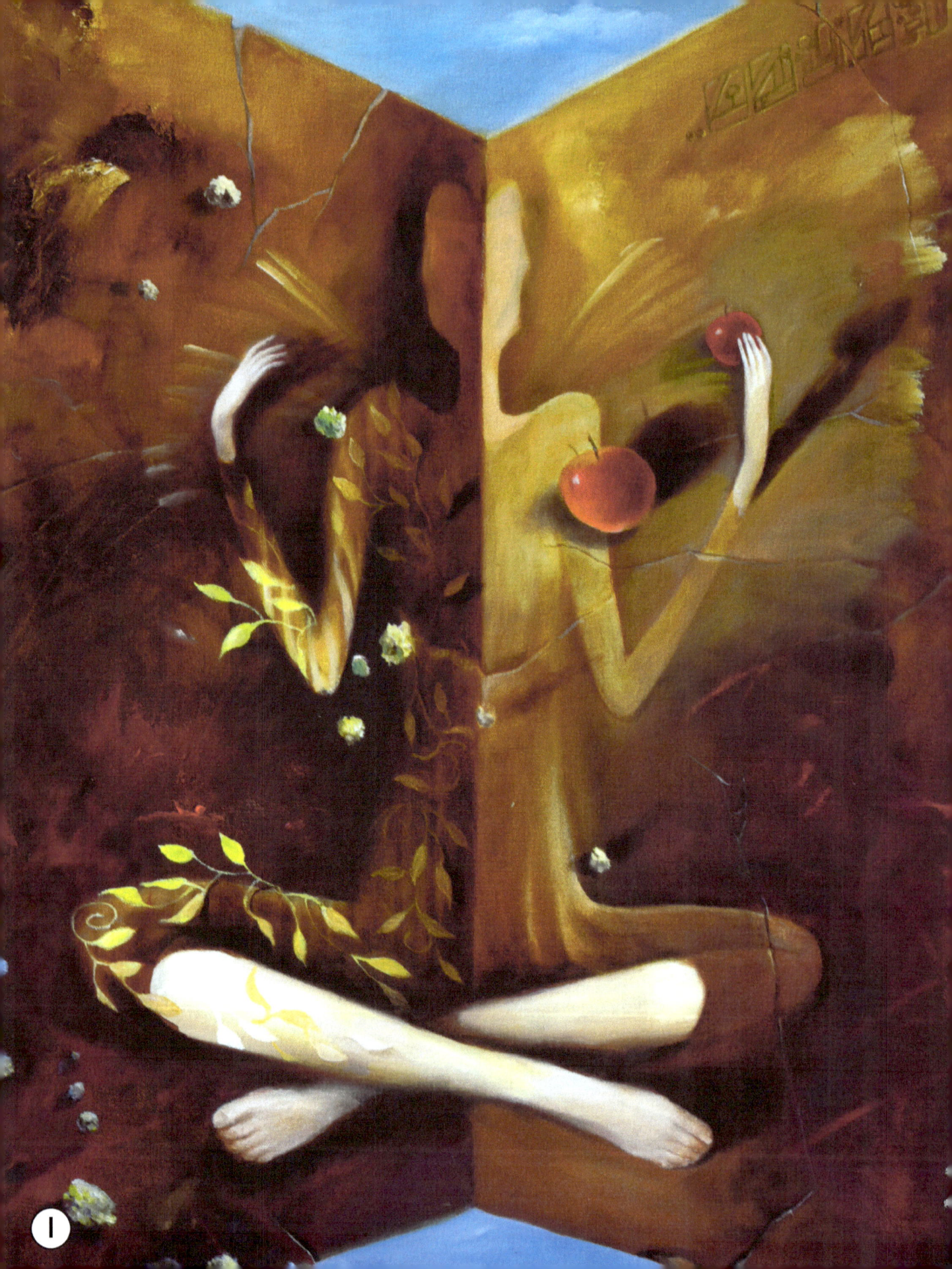

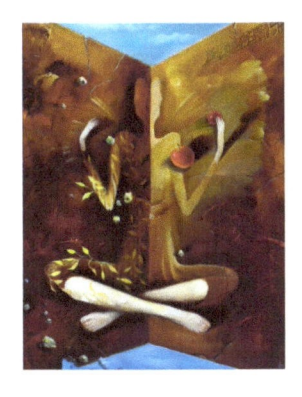

if asked
why they did that,

they would say:
out of conviction.

but what are their convictions?

rules attract rulers,
law creates lawyers,
demons provoke demonstrations –

language must be trusted.

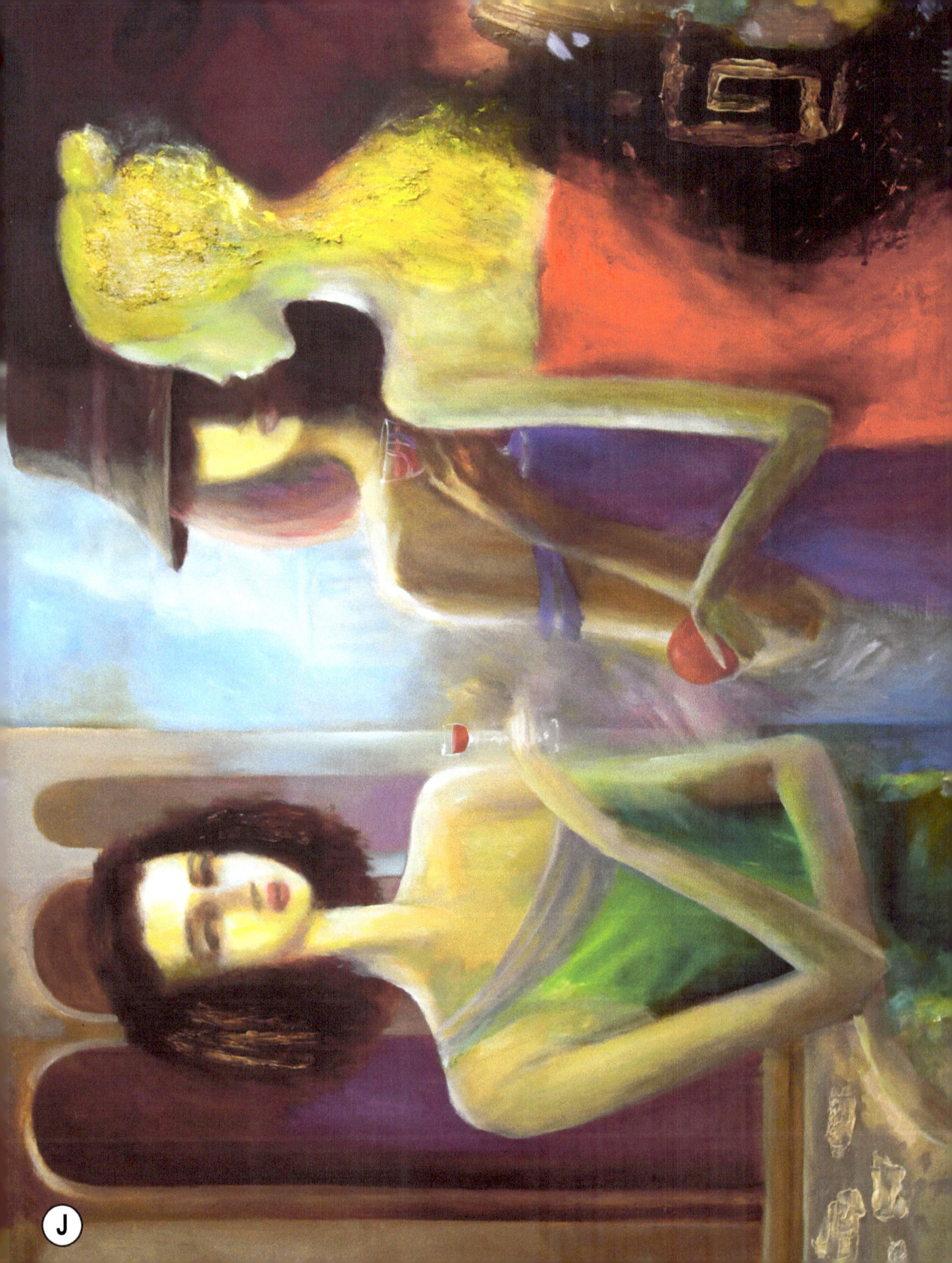

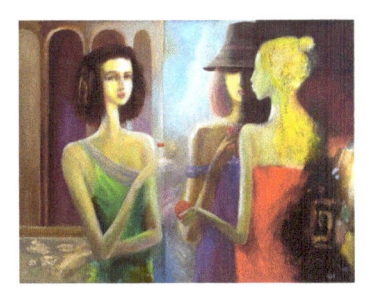

you've never met them –
yet you know
their looks and smiles.

you've never touched them –
yet you know
their sighs.

do not even try to recall
what dresses they were wearing,
what wine they drank,

those young women.

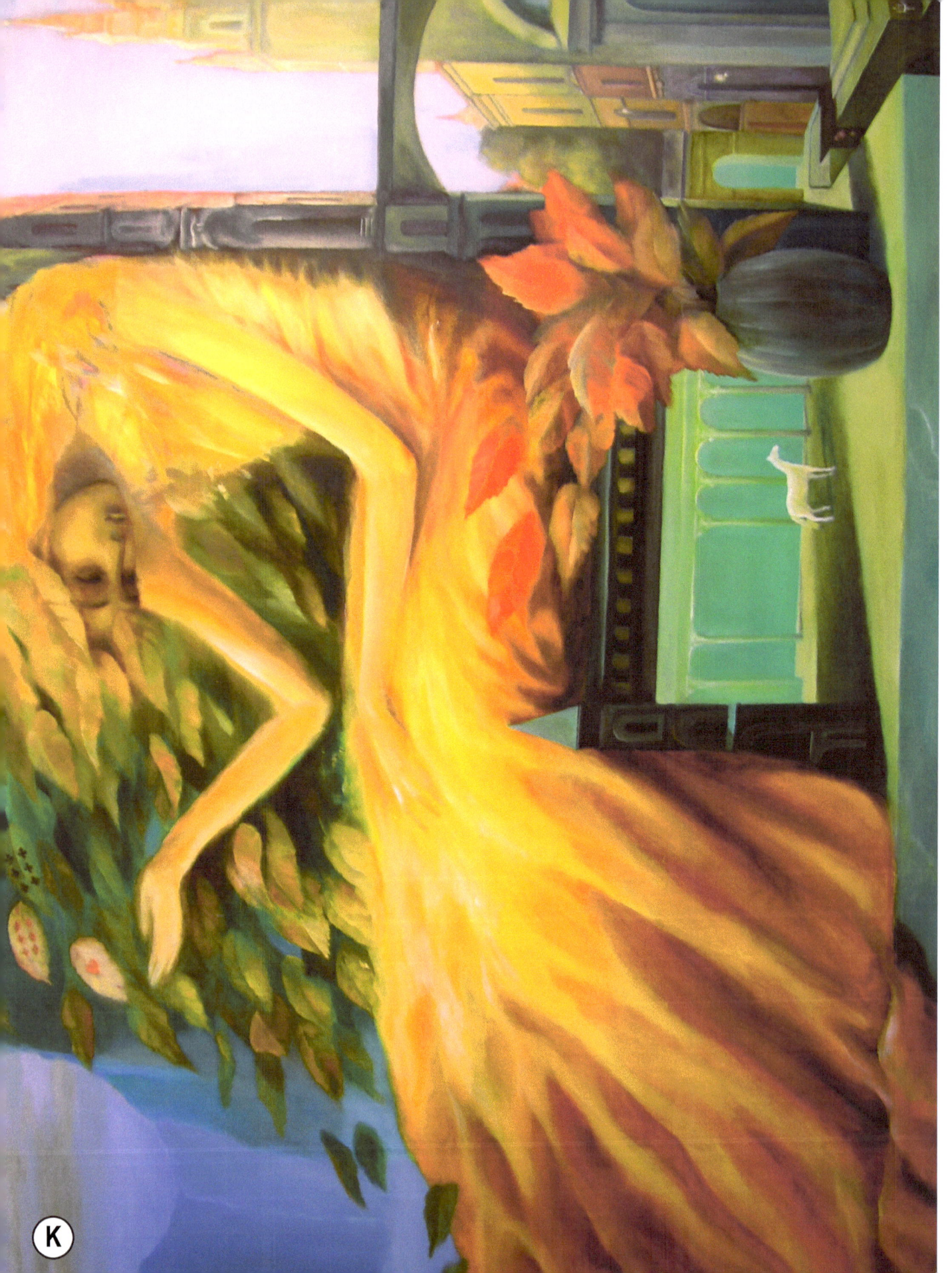

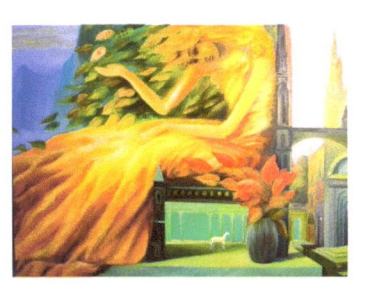

does it mean the game is over? –
intruders are everywhere.

yet things have not changed much:

trees feel a kind of relief,
animals too,

and plenty of old buildings
are unoccupied.

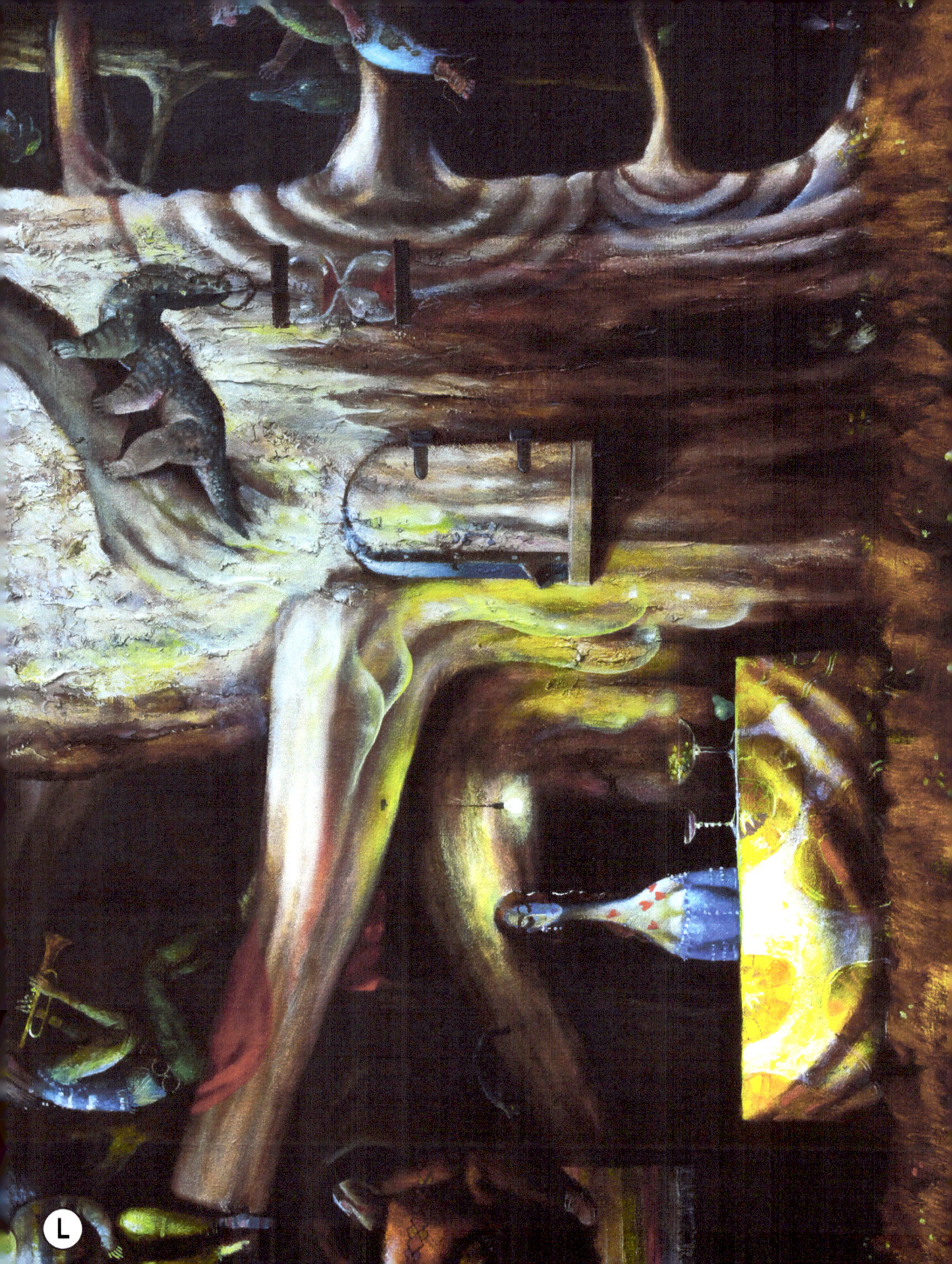

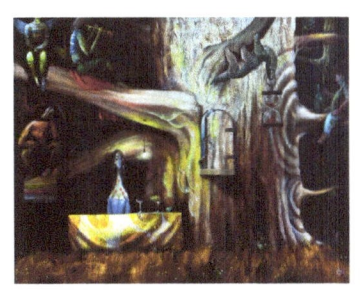

shall we pretend
nothing of importance is happening?

folks are hanging out
enjoying themselves
not worrying about
Nidhoggr messing with the roots of the Tree
or Ratatoskr reaching to the upper branches.

storyteller, shall we pretend
we still seek to know?

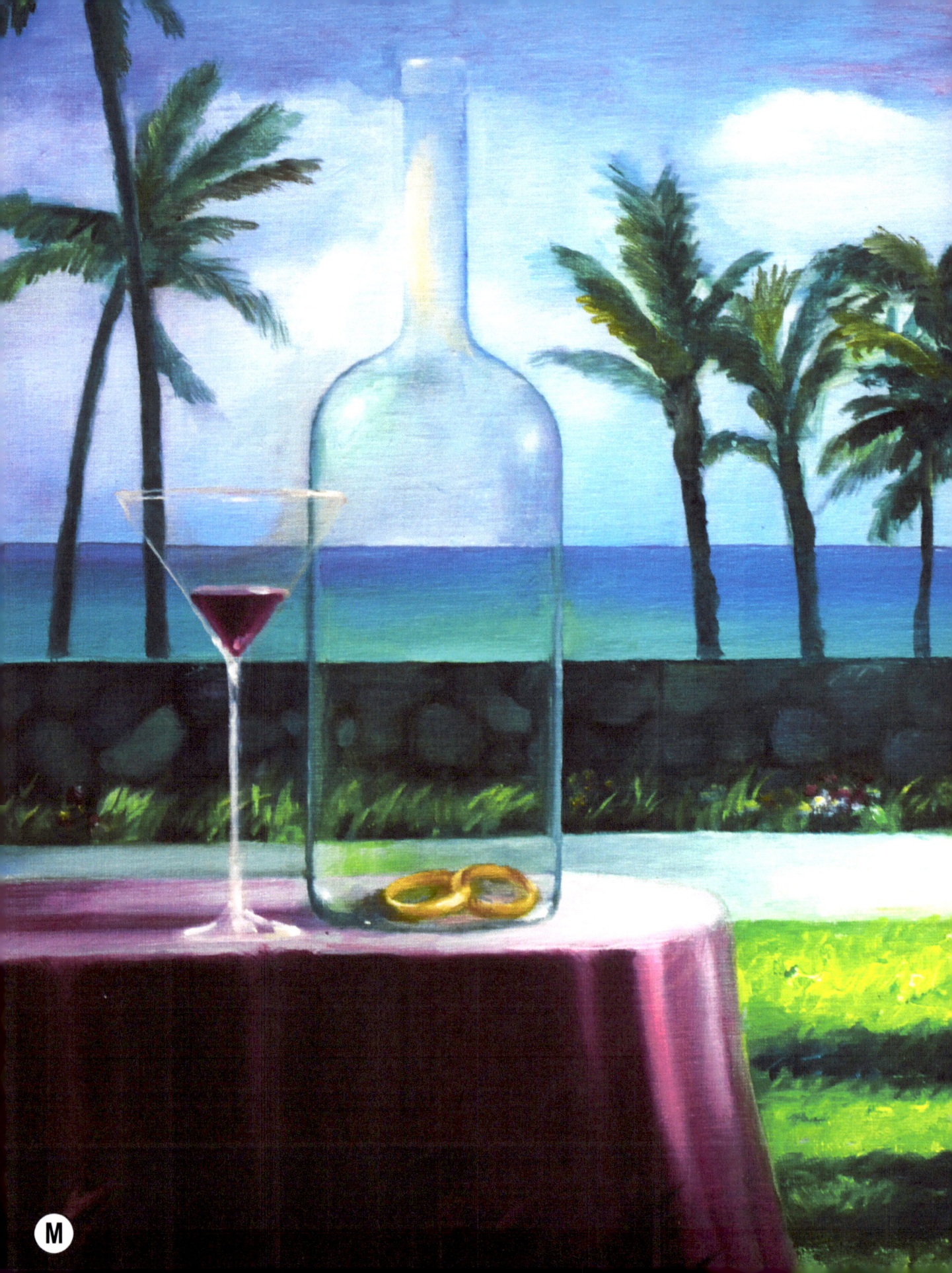

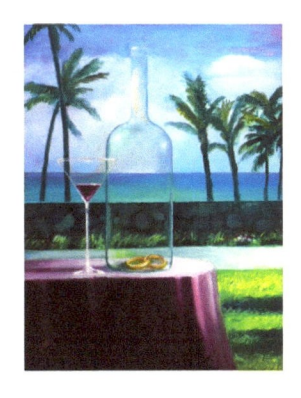

let us drink some wine
invoking the names
of Li Po and Du Fu.

don't be surprised
when you spot a second moon
or a third,

as you discover them
in the canvas
of an old master –

not in the night sky.

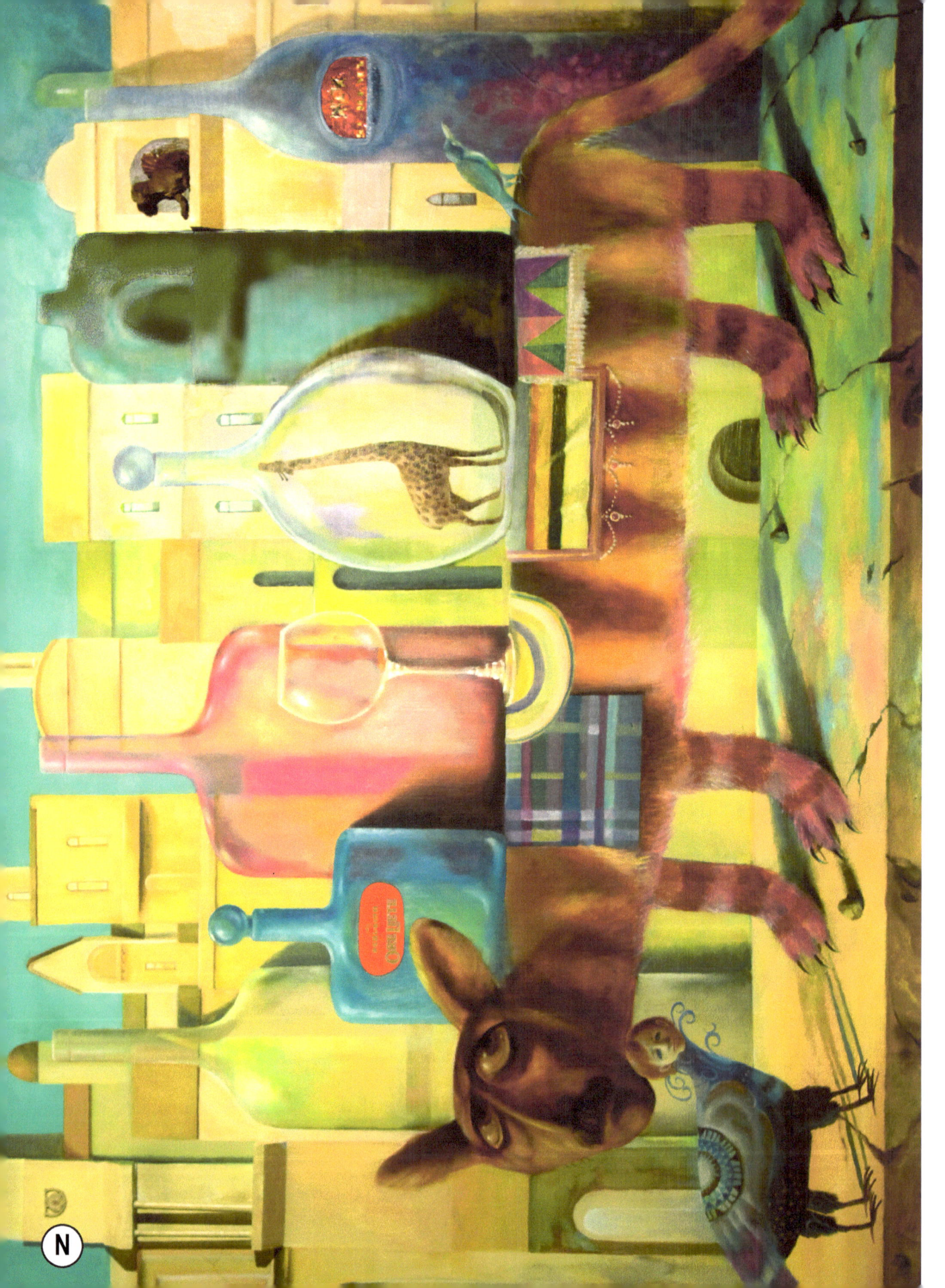

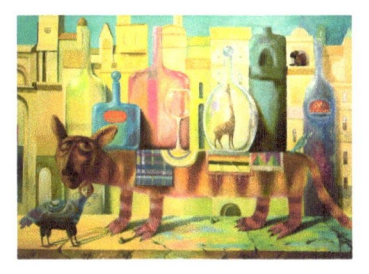

here we are, my friend,
here we are – in a zoo
of decoy-buildings and complicated jars.

it seems some objects
have a tendency
to grow legs and feathers.

the most stunning feature is the face,
nevertheless it does not take much effort
to acquire one –

just look around…

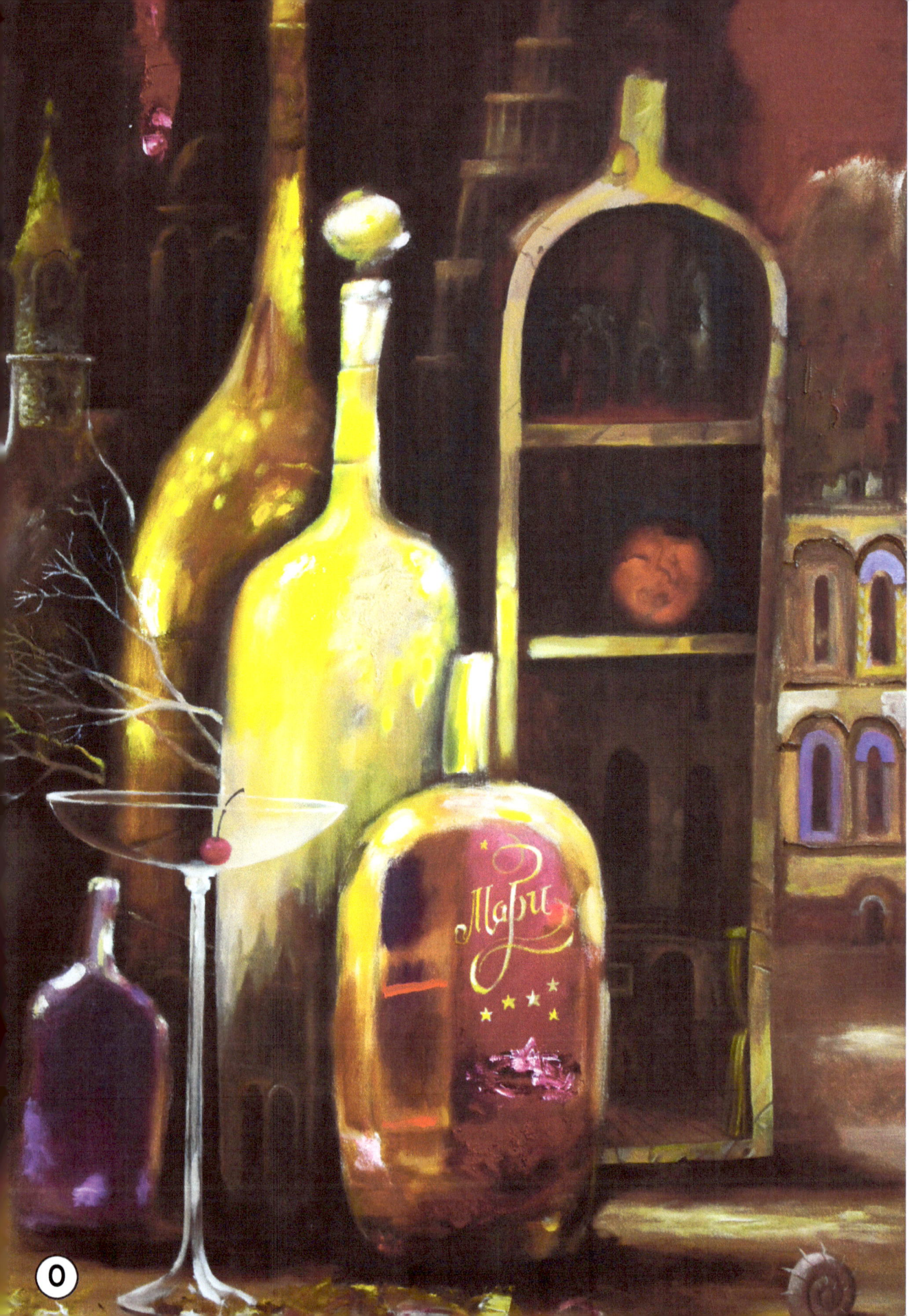

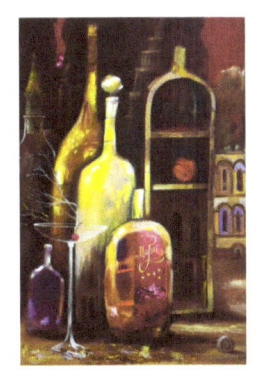

jars and bottles
are devouring the space
already compromised by gravity.

in the guise
of colors and shapes
they excrete an existential threat.

why people consort
with such monsters
is beyond understanding.

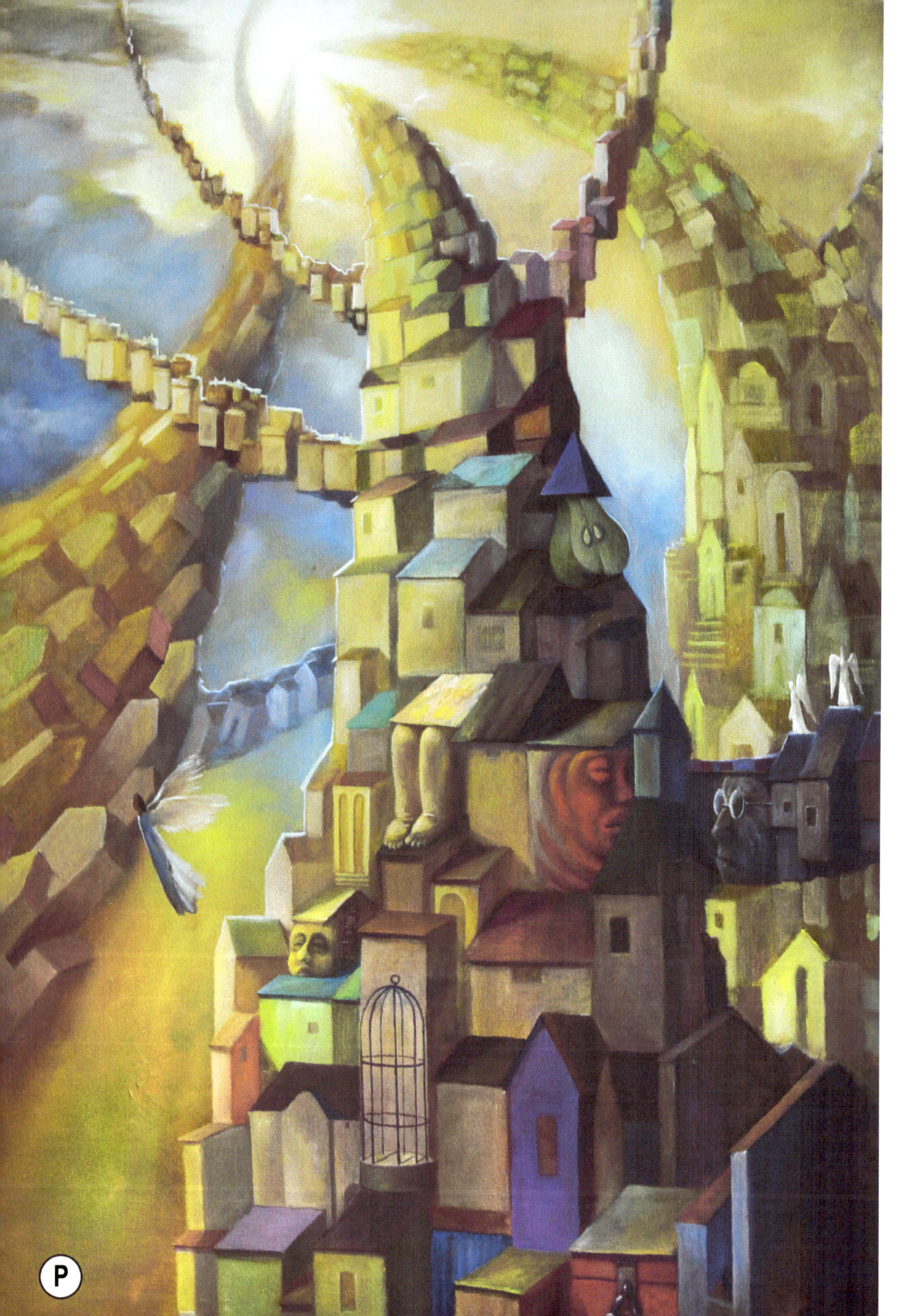

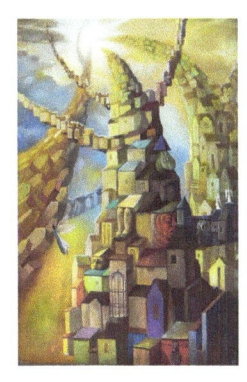

imagine a world
without straight lines
or right angles:

the earth
bringing forth towers
crooked as palms,

the sun
releasing ready icons –
not naked rays.

the inhabitants of such a world –
how pleasantly twisted
they would be!

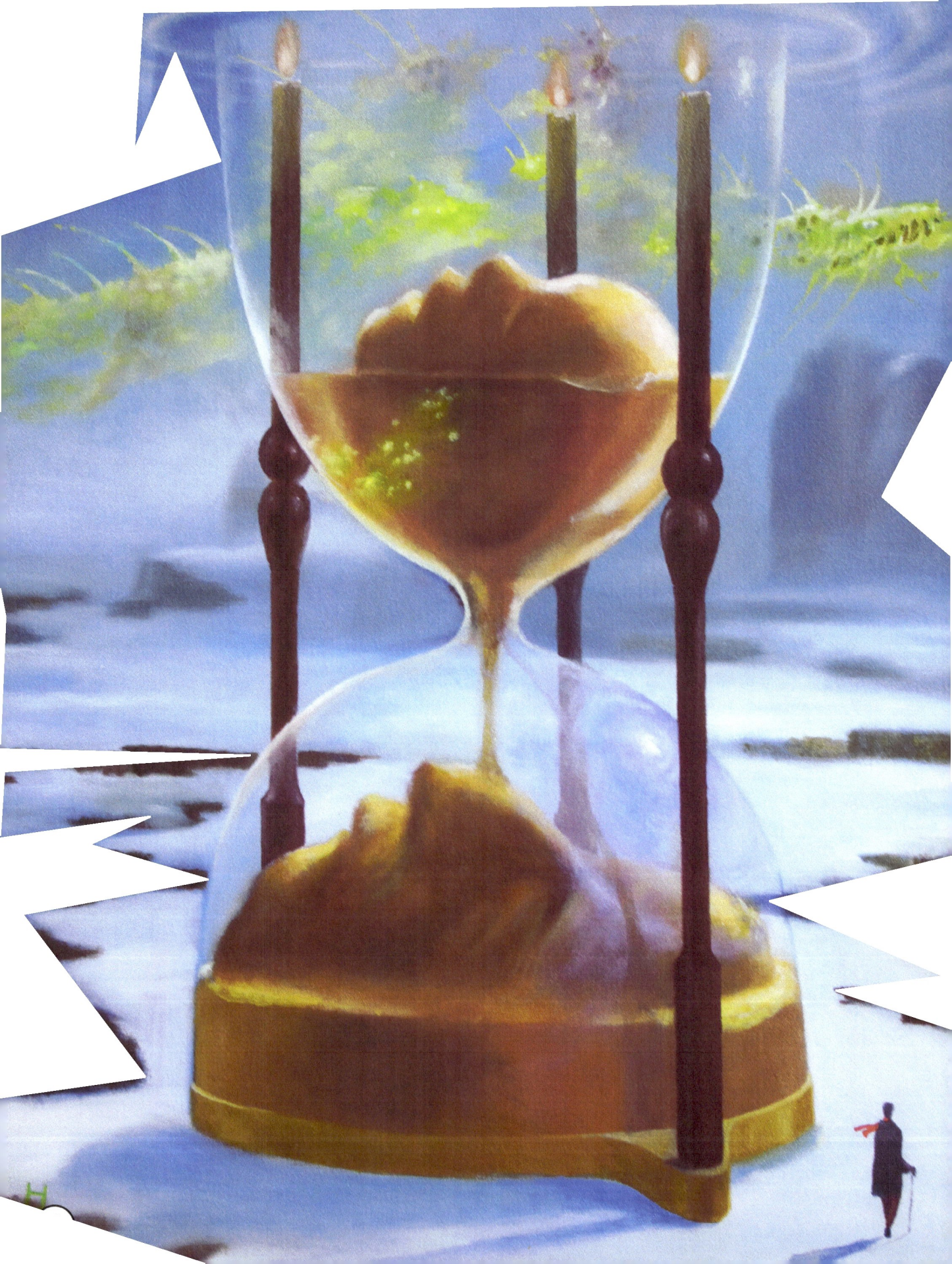

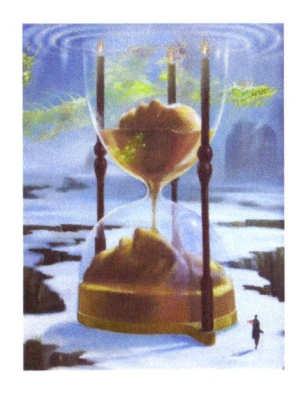

on ancestry-dot-com
a collection of well-worn masks
can be found.

it's all in your genes – they say
on once-story-dot-com.

eventually the beach sculpture
becomes a faceless dune.

nobody's out there to connect the dots.

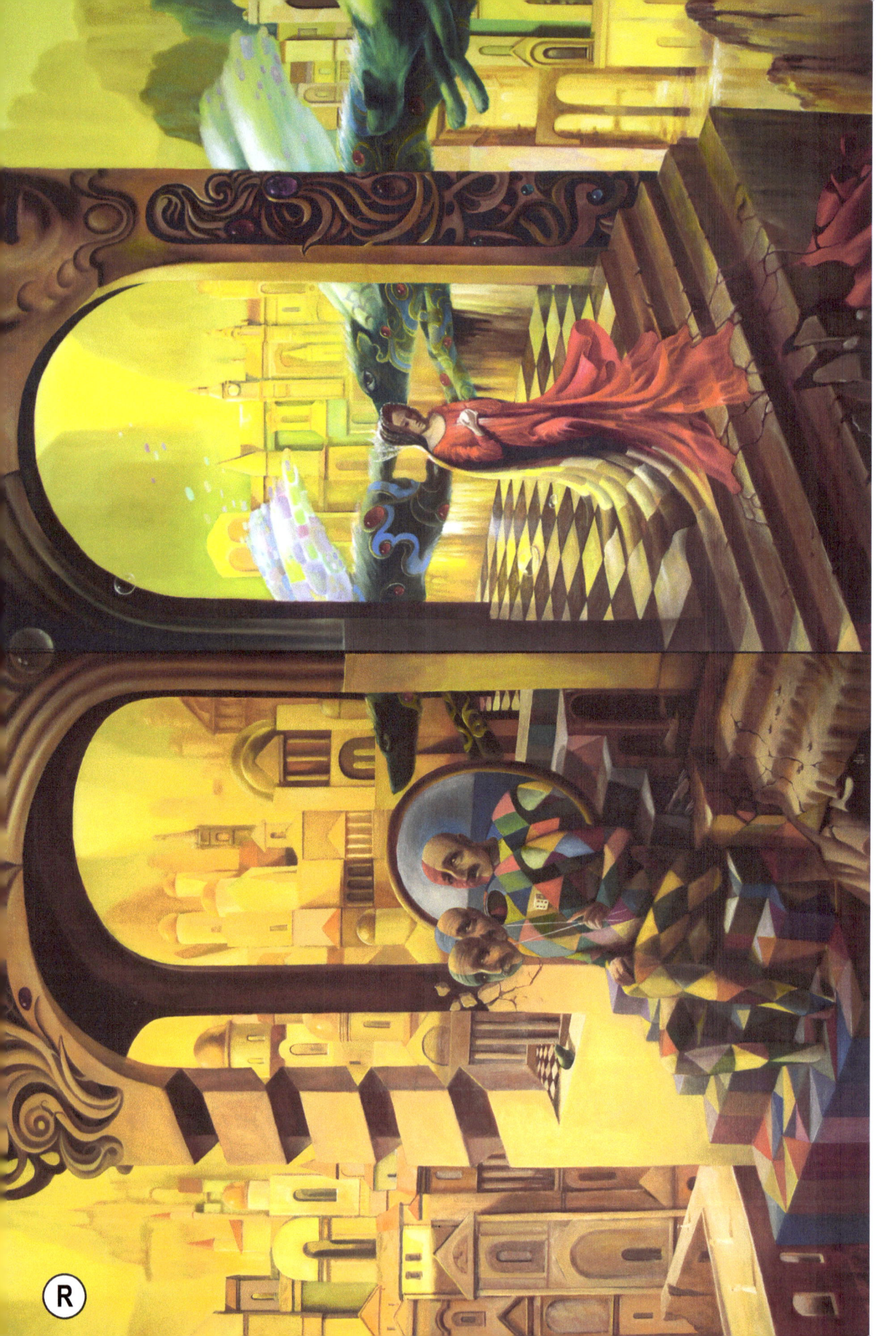

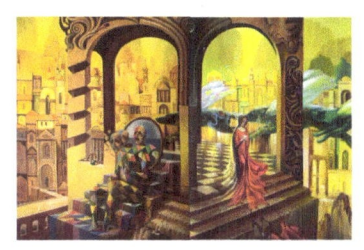

alien, resolute,
in military camouflage –
will they attack?

a few steps out of the palace
facing the unknown
she ceases to be the queen.

it is much safer
to stay inside
but she's made up her mind already.

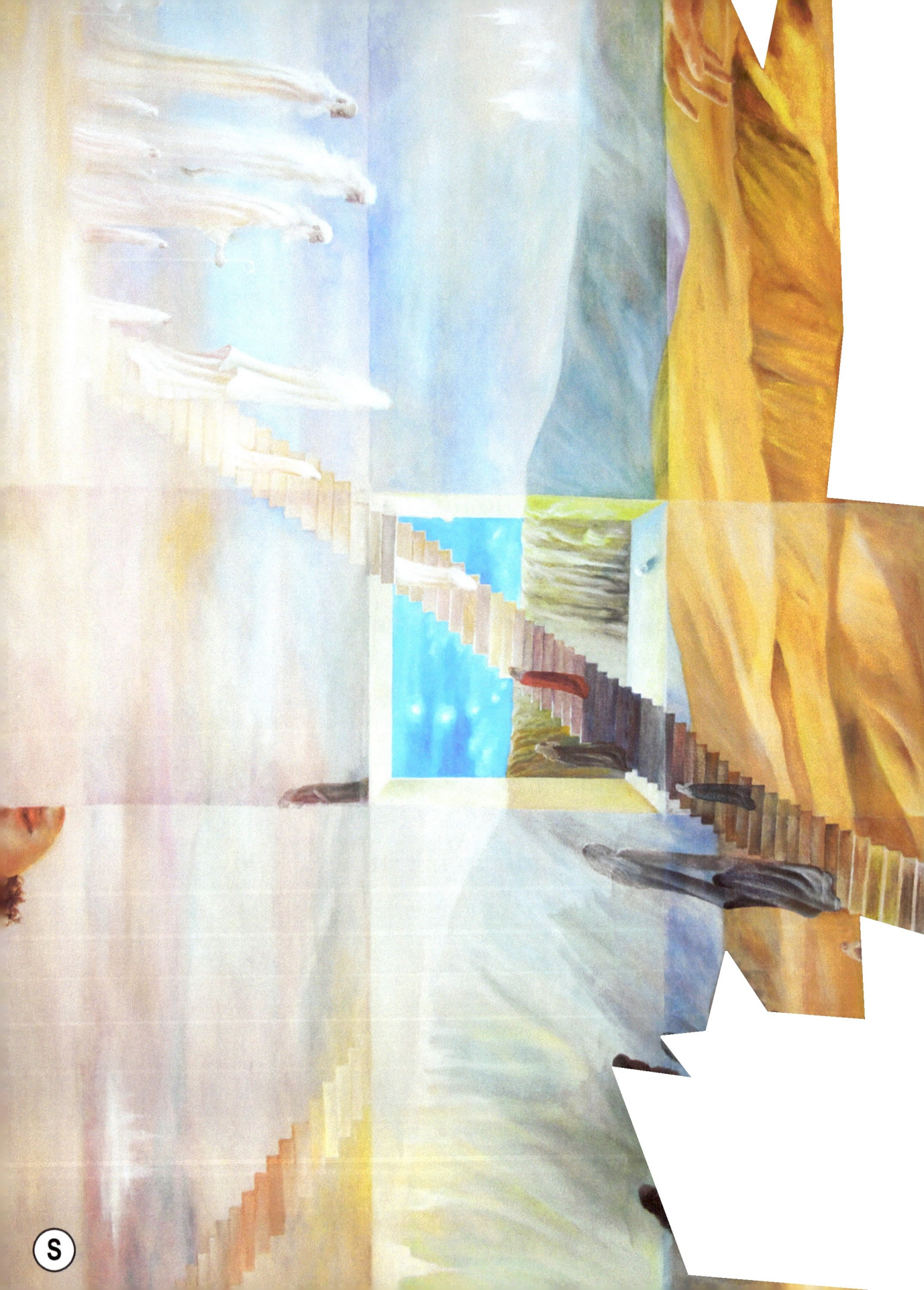

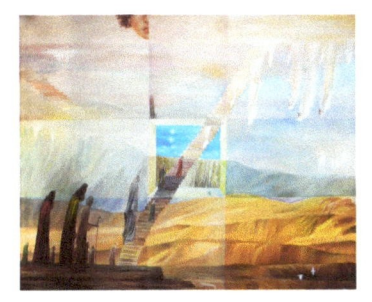

The Truth will set you free –
**if this is true
why are we still enslaved
by logic and prayer?**

**those eager to penetrate the mirror
and go beyond it
(arguably to heaven)
encounter a broken image.**

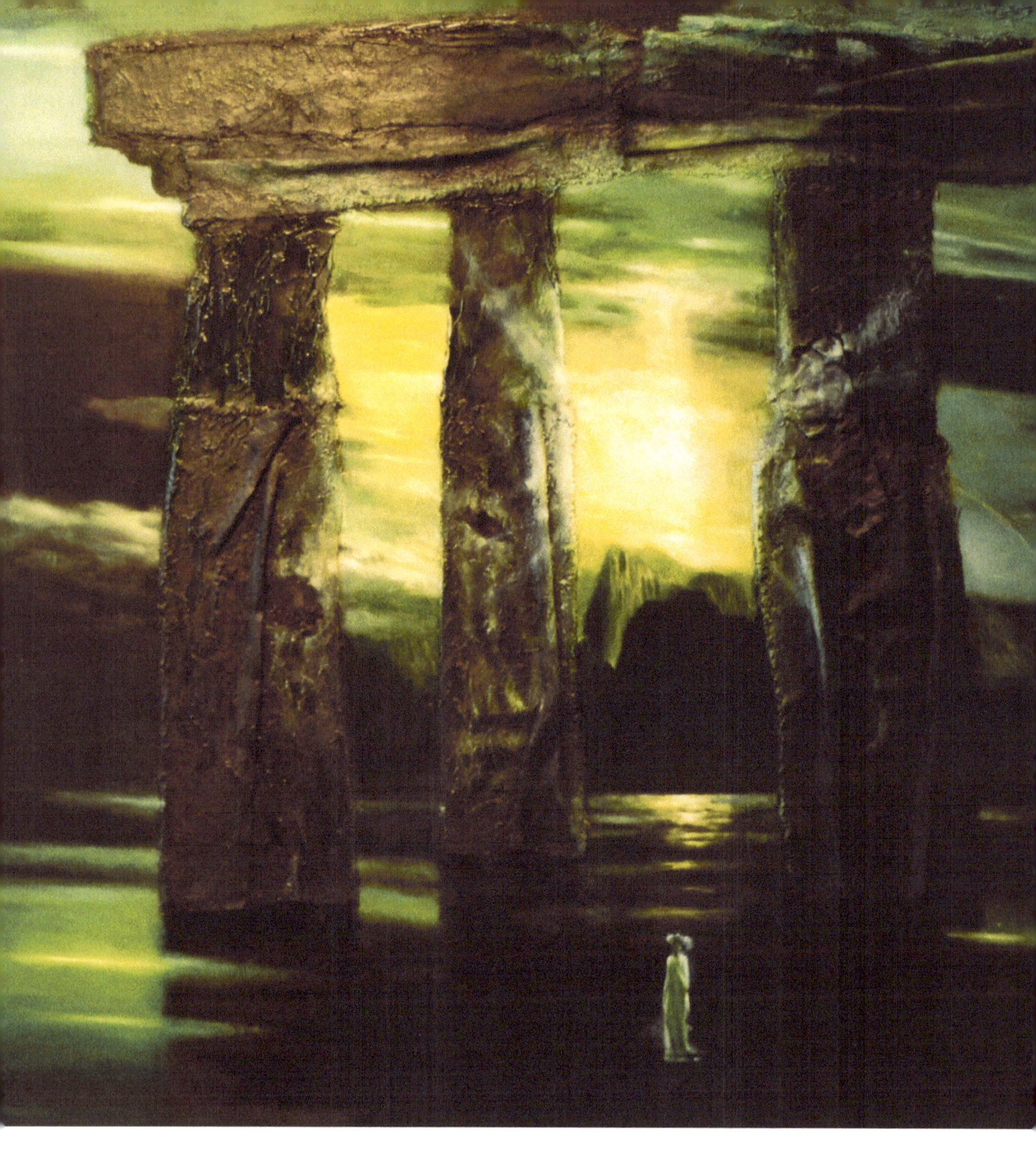

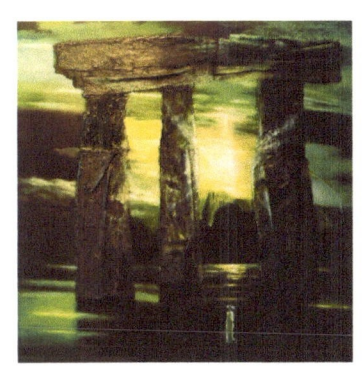

a search for meaning
is like a search
for a missing person:
exciting at the start,
almost hopeless in the end.

the erected stones
will do our bidding –
like a body
finally found,
in a sense resurrected.

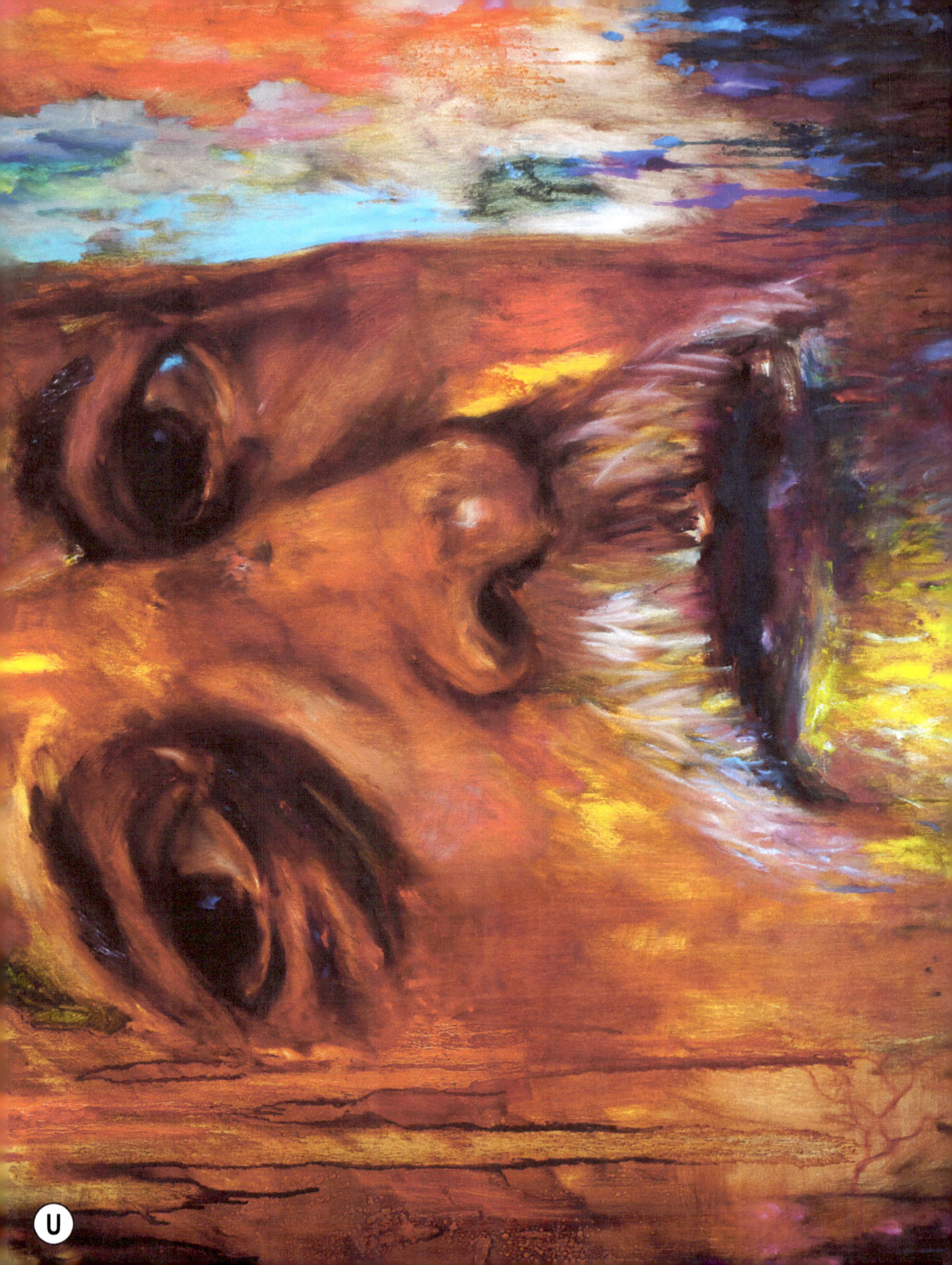

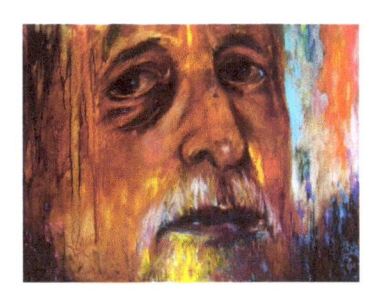

persistence of self-portraits!
every artist
has them.

a composer,
a poet,
a dancer –
they should be jealous!

but they aren't.

is that because self-awareness is
a two-dimensional illusion?

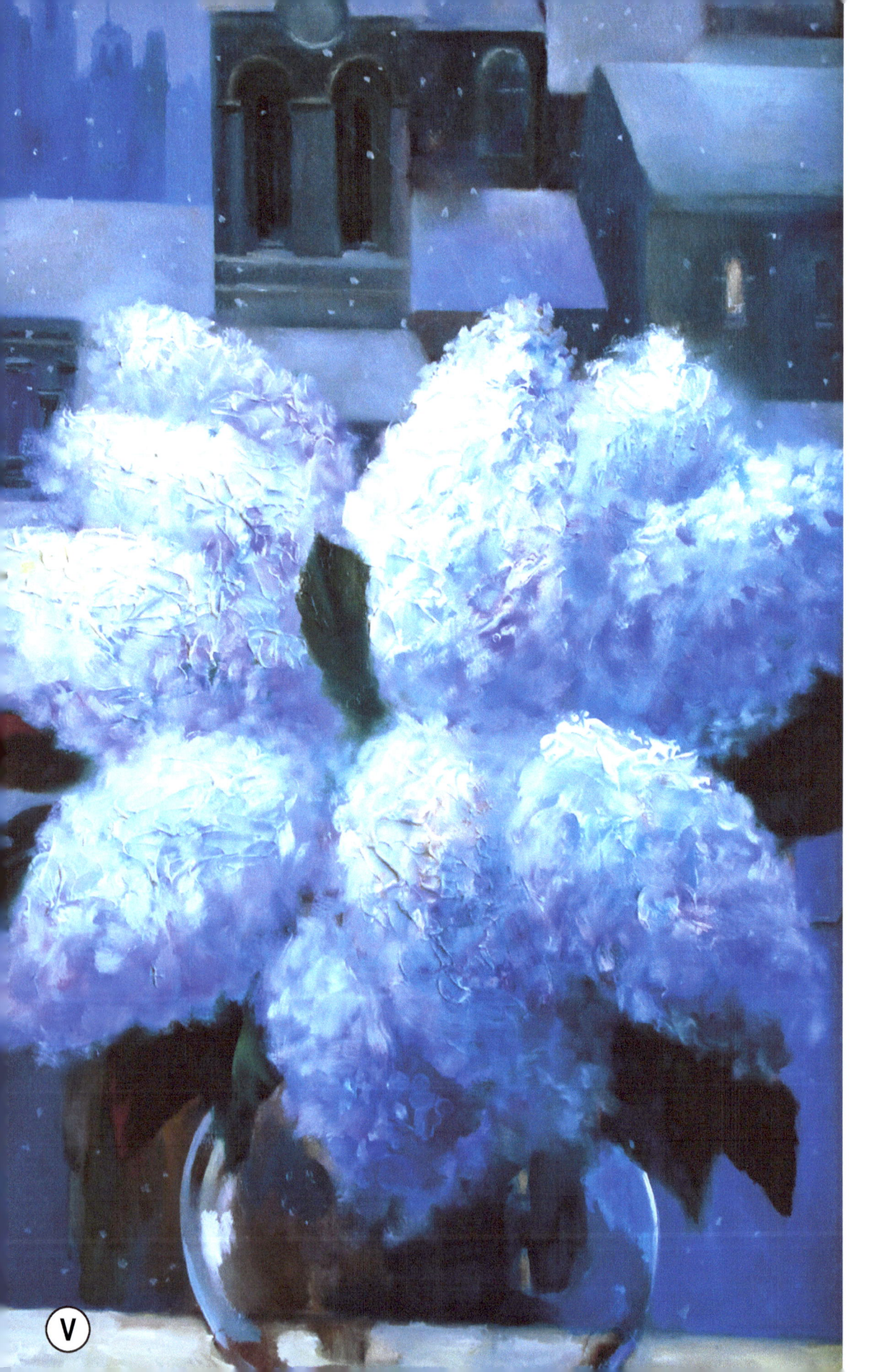

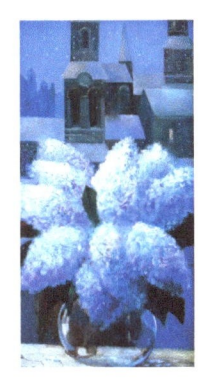

we are the link
between the flower's scent
and its Latin name,
between the taste of water
and the clouds above.

when an artist comes
with his stained easel
to paint flowers in a vase
he is not creating things –
he is fixing the link.

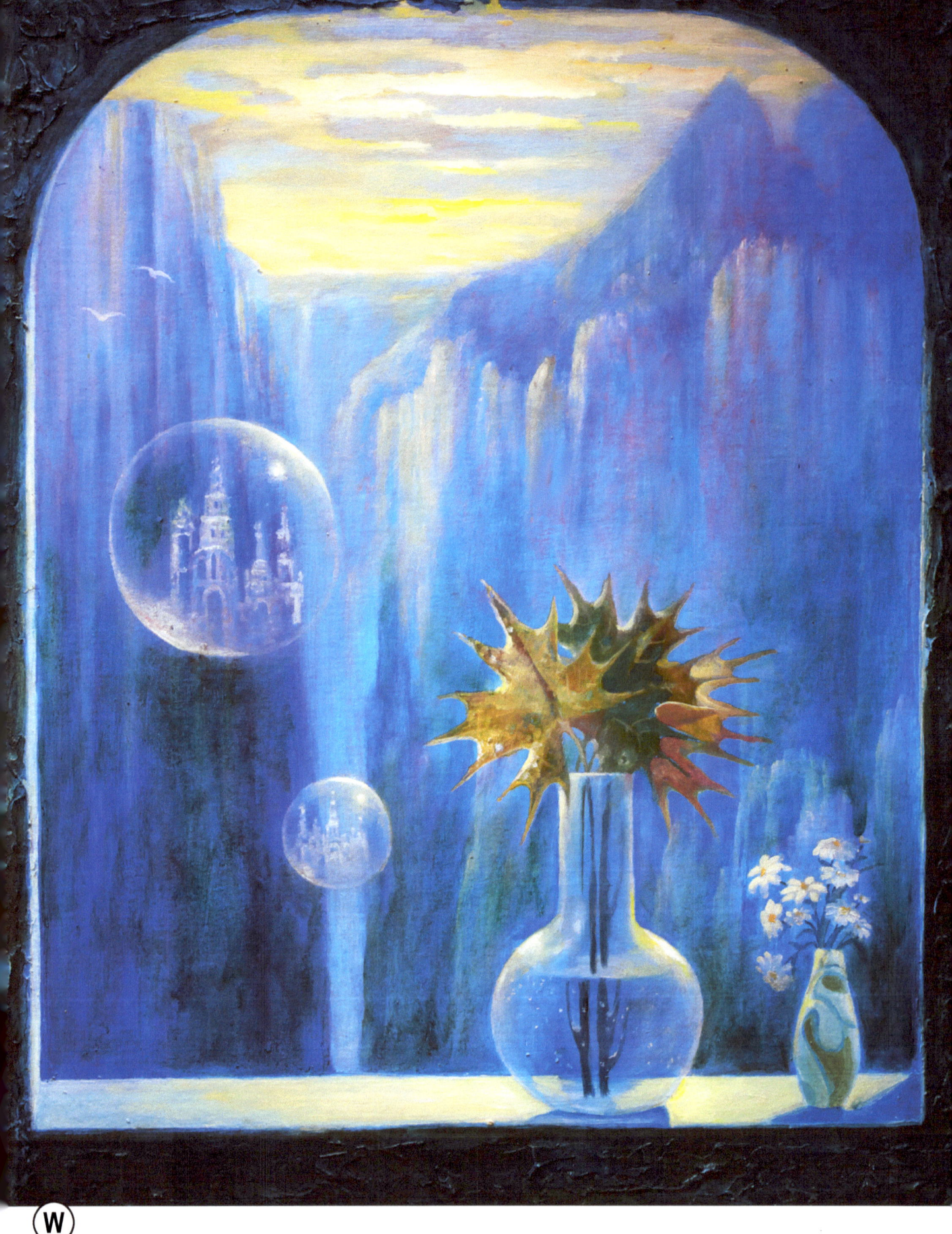

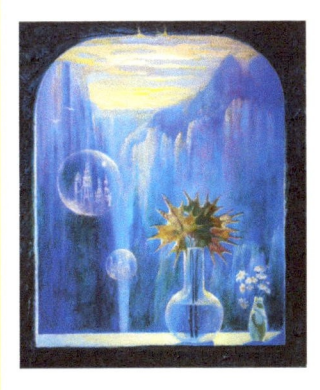

you can blow up a tower,
you can blow up *das Schloß*,
you can blow up the Kremlin
if it comes across.

you can do some damage
to the earth and the sky
or just blow a few bubbles
and let them fly.

53

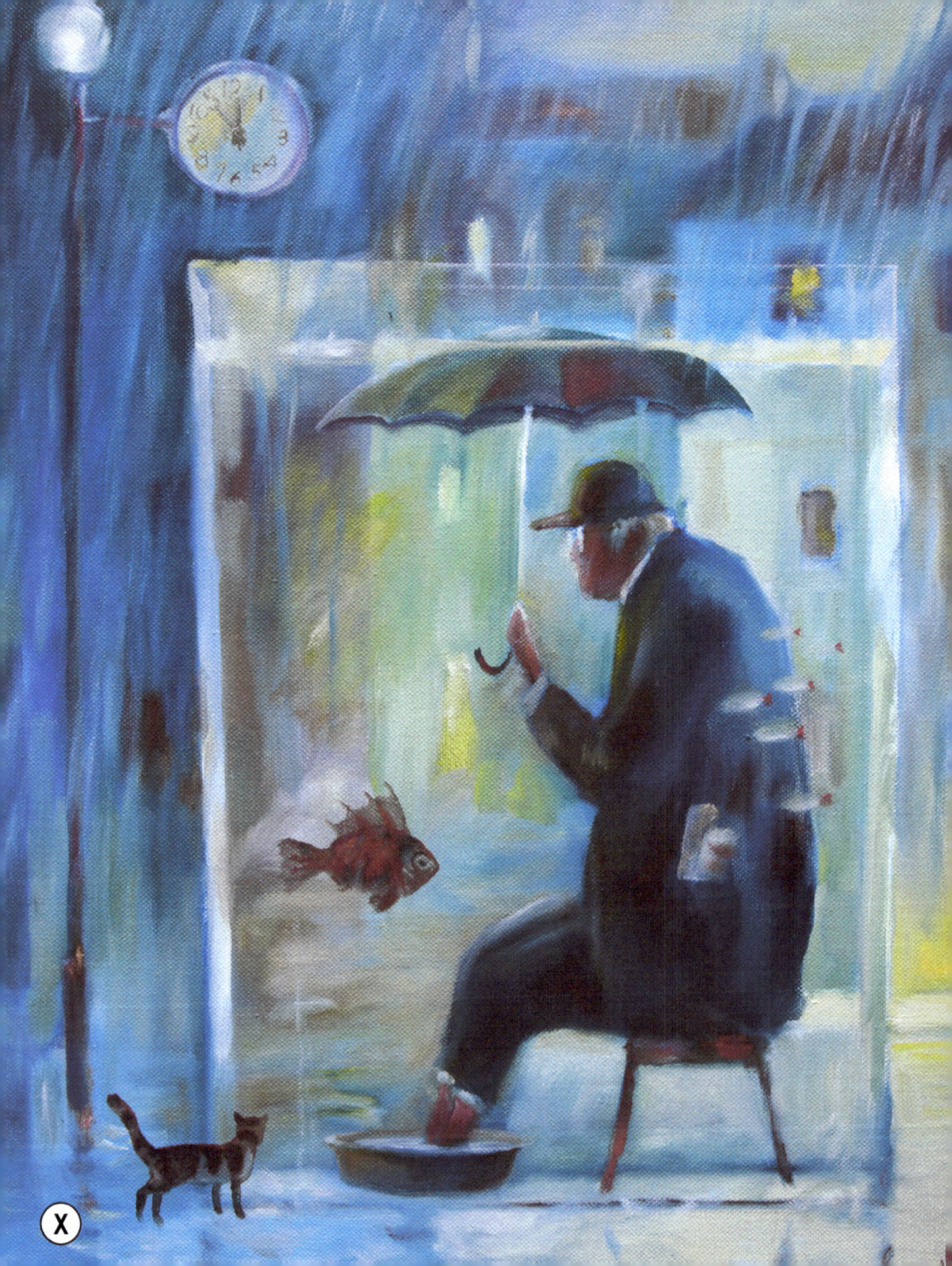

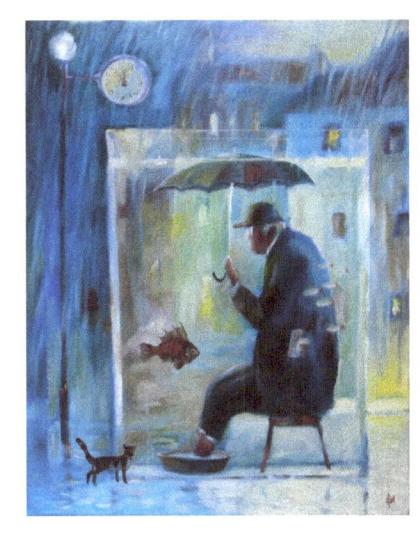

getting old…

sliding slowly to the bottom
of a huge aquarium
filled with wry hours.

calm down – the fish mutters –
welcome to our think-tank
(luckily no brainstorm on the horizon).

all *pollutics* are local.
get good umbrella insurance –
you'll be around for the long haul.

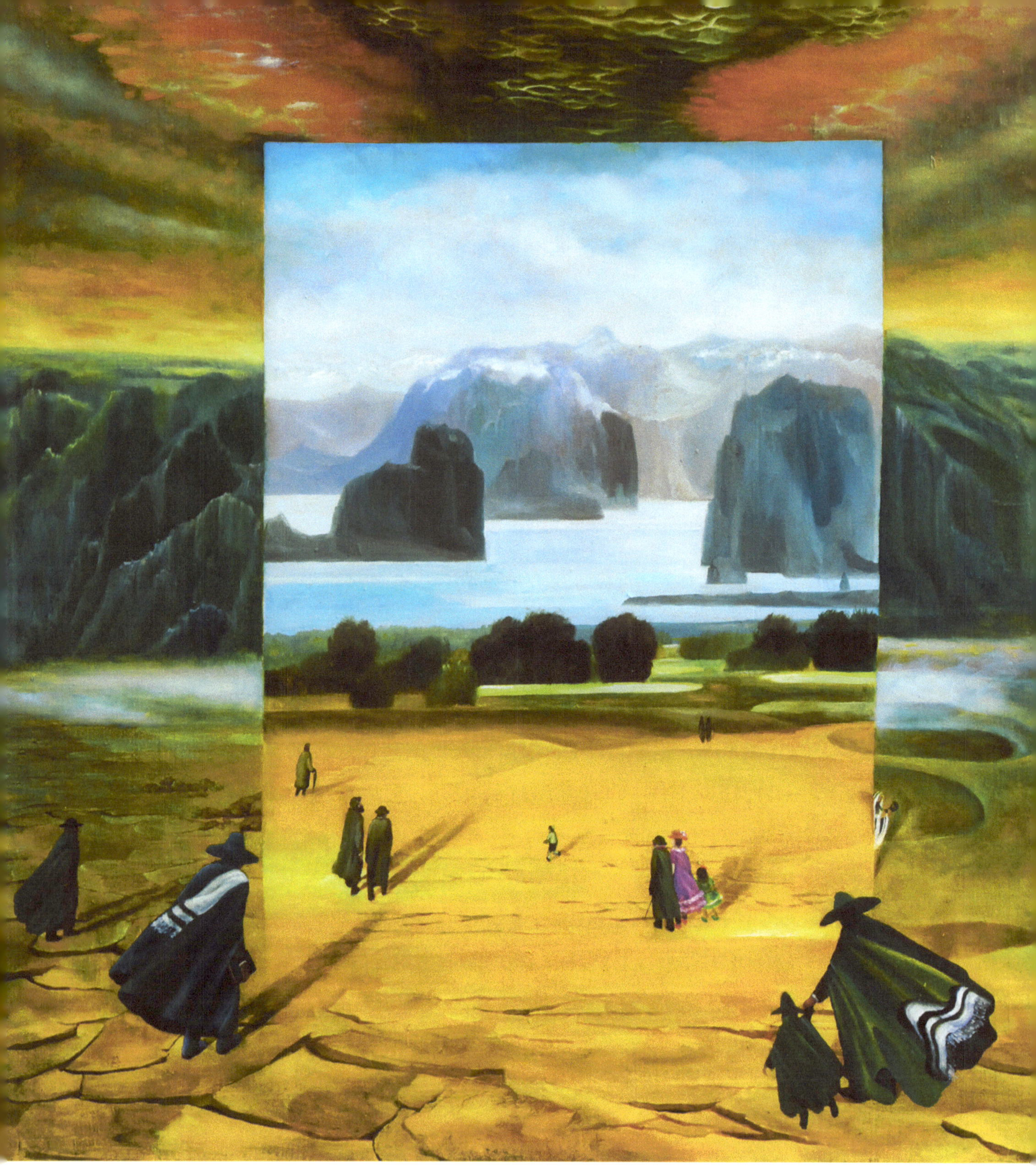

Y

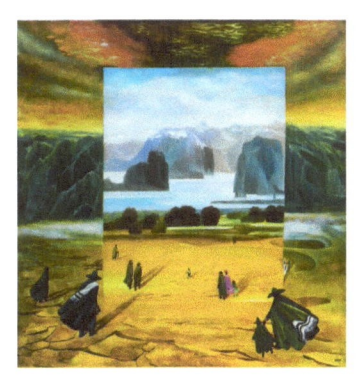

once
You split the Red Sea
for us to flee Egypt.

to escape the *Shoah*
the whole world
should have been split.

You excused yourself
from the action this time –
the artist did it.

but it was too late for too many.

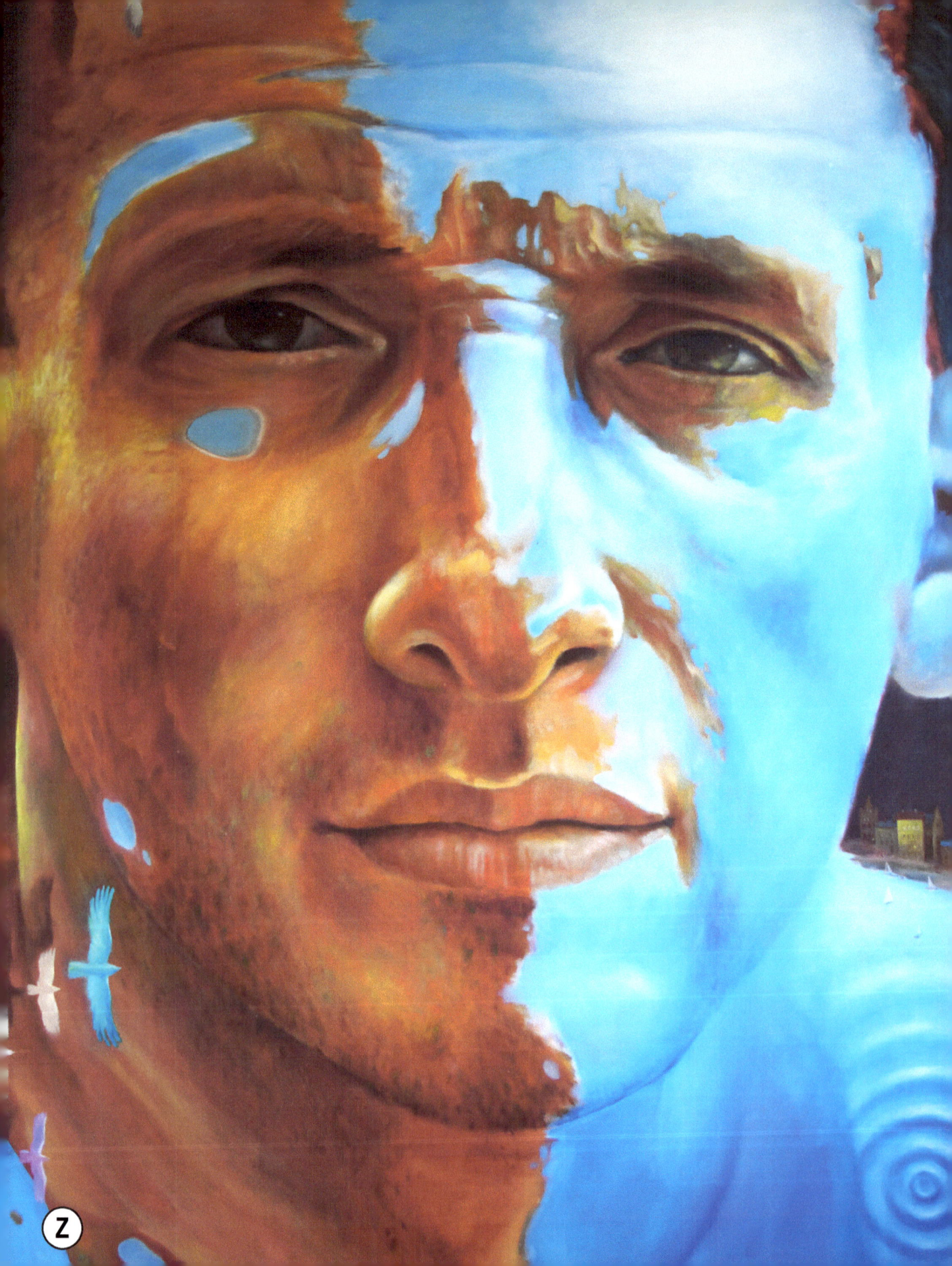

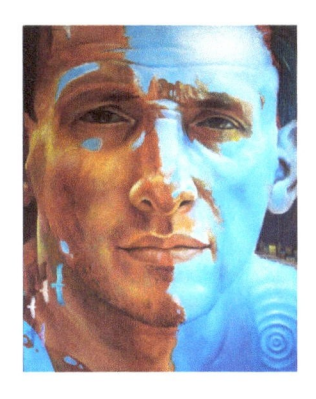

when you are a ballet dancer
you learn how to suffer –
Kristin Laidre asserts.

a poet suffers intuitively
yet needs training
in happiness.

hovering about a studio
a model learns
how to fly.

Notes:

page 30

The Tree - in North mythology the Tree of Existence, Yggdrasil.
According the Edda, among the creatures that live within Yggdrasil, are the Eagle, the wyrm (dragon) called Nidhoggr, gnawing its roots, and the squirrel called Ratatoskr scurries up and down, carrying messages between the Eagle and Nidhoggr.

page 32

Li Po and Du Fu – two greatest poets of China 8 century A.C. in the time of Tang Dynasty.

page 44

"the Truth will set you free" - (Veritas vos liberabit – Latin) – a quotation from the New Testament.

page 52

das Schloß (German) - the castle.

page 54

"pollutics" – a wordplay, combination of "politics" and 'pollution".

page 56

the Shoah (Hebrew) – Holocaust.

page 58

the quotation is taken from interview with Kristin Laidre ("Smithsonian", May 2009, page 32)

List of Artworks

A	Cellolana,	oil on canvas,	42" x 60",	2006
B	The Apple Garden	oil on canvas,	36" x 48",	2008
C	Queen of the Game II	oil on canvas,	30" x 40",	2008
D	Jungle	oil on canvas,	30" x 40",	2008
E	Barbara with the Flute	oil on canvas,	24" x 36",	2006
F	Evening	oil on canvas,	24" x 36",	2009
G	Queen of the Game I	oil on canvas,	30" x 40",	2007
H	Dialogue	oil on canvas,	52" x 72",	2007
I	Prisoner of the Soul	oil on canvas,	22" x 28",	2007
J	Three Girls	oil on canvas,	40" x 30",	2008
K	Fall	oil on canvas,	40" x 30",	2008
L	Man in her Life	oil on canvas,	35" x 27",	2006
M	Cancun	oil on canvas,	16" x 20",	2007
N	Bottles	mixed-media,	48" x 36",	2009
O	Bottles at Night	oil on canvas,	24" x 36",	2006
P	Sunny Trees	oil on canvas,	24" x 36",	2008
Q	Sand Watch	oil on canvas,	22" x 24",	2006
R	Vlad's City	oil on canvas,	96" x 60",	2007
S	Symmetrical World	oil on canvas,	52" x 42",	2006
T	Stonehenge	mixed-media,	48" x 48",	2005
U	Self-portrait in red	oil on canvas,	48" x 36",	2008
V	Winter Flowers	oil on board,	14" x 31",	2009
W	The Bubble World	mixed-media,	22" x 28",	2007
X	The Rain	oil on canvas,	16" x 20",	2009
Y	Invitation to Synagogue	oil on canvas,	36" x 36",	2002
Z	Matthew's Planet	oil on canvas,	48" x 60",	2009

TRANSCENDING IMAGES

Art, Poetry